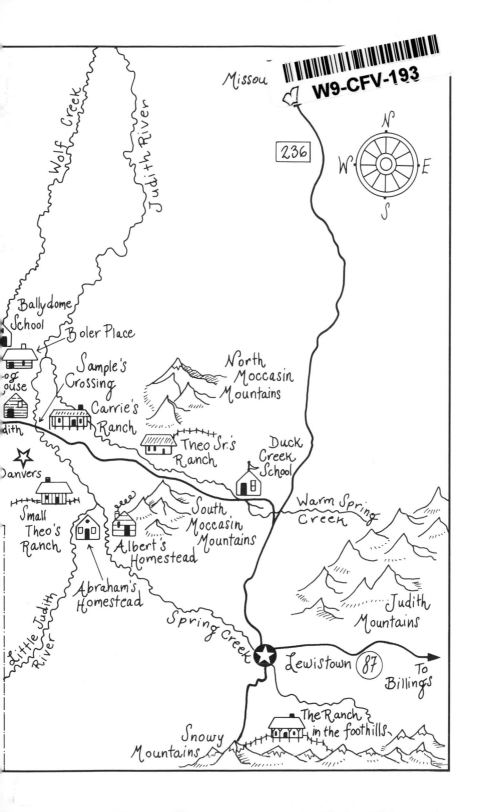

Missou...

236

W9-CFV-193

N
W   E
S

Wolf Creek

Judith River

Ballydome
School

Boler Place

Sample's
Crossing

Carrie's
Ranch

North
Moccasin
Mountains

og
ouse

dith

Theo Sr.'s
Ranch

Duck
Creek
School

Danvers

Small
Theo's
Ranch

Albert's
Homestead

South
Moccasin
Mountains

Warm Spring
Creek

Judith
Mountains

Abraham's
Homestead

Little Judith River

Spring Creek

Lewistown 87

To
Billings

Snowy
Mountains

The Ranch
in the foothills.

December 1992

Merry Christmas to Mother,
who loves Montana - its freedom and
possibilities and rawness.
Love,
Katherine

ALL BUT
THE WALTZ

ALL BUT
THE WALTZ

ESSAYS ON A MONTANA FAMILY

Mary Clearman Blew

VIKING

VIKING
Published by the Penguin Group
Viking Penguin, a division of Penguin Books USA Inc.,
375 Hudson Street, New York, New York 10014, U.S.A.
Penguin Books Ltd, 27 Wrights Lane, London W8 5TZ, England
Penguin Books Australia Ltd, Ringwood, Victoria, Australia
Penguin Books Canada Ltd, 10 Alcorn Avenue, Suite 300,
Toronto, Ontario, Canada M4V 3B2
Penguin Books (N.Z.) Ltd, 182-190 Wairau Road, Auckland 10, New Zealand

Penguin Books Ltd, Registered Offices: Harmondsworth, Middlesex, England

First published in 1991 by Viking Penguin, a division of Penguin Books USA Inc.

3 5 7 9 10 8 6 4 2

LIBRARY OF CONGRESS CATALOGING IN PUBLICATION DATA
Blew, Mary Clearman
All but the waltz : essays on a Montana family / Mary Clearman Blew.
p.   cm.
ISBN 0–670–83108–5
1. Judith River Valley (Mont.)—Social life and customs.
2. Judith River Valley (Mont.)—Biography.
3. Clearman family.
4. Blew, Mary Clearman, 1939– —Biography—Family.
5. Authors, American—20th century—Biography—Family.
I. Title. F737.J83B57   1991
978.6'62—dc20   91-50145

Printed in the United States of America
Set in Sabon
Designed by Jessica Shatan
Map by Virginia Norey

For Elizabeth

CONTENTS

ALL BUT
THE WALTZ

THE SOW IN
THE RIVER

Spring Creek, about 1900.

| | | | | | | | | | | | | | | | | | | | | | | | | | | | | | | | | | | | | | | | | | |

In the sagebrush to the north of the mountains in central Montana, where the Judith River deepens its channel and threads a slow, treacherous current between the cutbanks, a cottonwood log house still stands. It is in sight of the highway, about a mile downriver on a gravel road. From where I have turned off and stopped my car on the sunlit shoulder of the highway, I can see the house, a distant and solitary dark interruption of the sagebrush. I can even see the lone box elder tree, a dusty green shade over what used to be the yard.

I know from experience that if I were to keep driving over the cattle guard and follow the gravel road through the sage and alkali to the log house, I would find the windows gone and the door sagging and the floor rotting away. But from here the house looks hardly changed from the summer of my earliest memories, the summer before I was three, when I lived in that log house on the lower Judith with my mother and father and grandmother and my grandmother's boyfriend, Bill.

My memories seem to me as treacherous as the river. Is it possible, sitting here on this dry shoulder of a secondary highway in the middle of Montana where the brittle weeds of August scratch at the sides of the car, watching the narrow blue Judith take its time to thread and wind through the bluffs on its way to a distant northern blur, to believe in anything but today? The past eases away with the current. I cannot watch a single drop of water out of sight. How can I trust memory, which slips and wobbles and grinds its erratic furrows like a bald-tired truck fighting for traction on a wet gumbo road?

| | | | | | |

Light flickers. A kerosene lamp in the middle of the table has driven the shadows back into the corners of the kitchen. Faces and hands emerge in a circle. Bill has brought apples from the box in the dark closet. The coil of peel follows his pocket-knife. I bite into the piece of quartered apple he hands me. I hear its snap, taste the juice. The shadows hold threats: mice and the shape of nameless things. But in the circle around the lamp, in the certainty of apples, I am safe.

The last of the kerosene tilts and glitters around the wick. I cower behind Grammy on the stairs, but she boldly walks into the shadows, which reel and retreat from her and her lamp. In her bedroom the window reflects large pale her and timorous me. She undresses herself, undresses me; she piles my pants and stockings on the chair with her dress and corset. After she uses it, her pot is warm for me. Her bed is cold, then warm. I burrow against her back and smell the smoke from the wick she has pinched out. Bill blows his nose from his bedroom on the other side of the landing. Beyond the eaves the shapeless creatures of sound, owls and coyotes, have taken the night. But I am here, safe in the center.

I am in the center again on the day we look for Bill's pigs. I am sitting between him and Grammy in the cab of the old

Ford truck while the rain sheets on the windshield. Bill found the pigpen gate open when he went to feed the pigs this morning, their pen empty, and now they are nowhere to be found. He has driven and driven through the sagebrush and around the gulches, peering out through the endless gray rain as the truck spins and growls on the gumbo in low gear. But no pigs. He and Grammy do not speak. The cab is cold, but I am bundled well between them with my feet on the clammy assortment of tools and nails and chains on the floorboards and my nose just dashboard level, and I am at home with the smell of wet wool and metal and the feel of a broken spring in the seat.

But now Bill tramps on the brakes, and he and Grammy and I gaze through the streaming windshield at the river. The Judith has risen up its cutbanks, and its angry gray current races the rain. I have never seen such a Judith, such a tumult of water. But what transfixes me and Grammy and Bill behind our teeming glass is not the ruthless condition of the river— no, for on a bare ait at midcurrent, completely surrounded and only inches above that muddy roiling water, huddle the pigs.

The flat top of the ait is so small that the old sow takes up most of it by herself. The river divides and rushes around her, rising, practically at her hooves. Surrounding her, trying to crawl under her, snorting in apprehension at the water, are her little pigs. Watching spellbound from the cab of the truck, I can feel their small terrified rumps burrowing against her sides, drawing warmth from her center even as more dirt crumbles under their hooves. My surge of understanding arcs across the current, and my flesh shrivels in the icy sheets of rain. Like the pigs I cringe at the roar of the river, although behind the insulated walls of the cab I can hear and feel nothing. I am in my center and they are in theirs. The current separates us irrevocably, and suddenly I understand that my center is as precarious as theirs, that the chill metal cab of the old truck is almost as fragile as their ring of crumbling sod.

And then the scene darkens and I see no more.

| | | | | | |

For years I would watch for the ait. When I was five my family moved, but I learned to snatch a glimpse whenever we drove past our old turnoff on the road from Lewistown to Denton. The ait was in plain view, just a hundred yards downriver from the highway, as it is today. *Ait* was a fancy word I learned afterward. It was a fifteen-foot-high steep-sided, flat-topped pinnacle of dirt left standing in the bed of the river after years of wind and water erosion. And I never caught sight of it without the same small thrill of memory: that's where the pigs were.

One day I said it out loud. I was grown by then. "That's where the pigs were."

My father was driving. We would have crossed the Judith River bridge, and I would have turned my head to keep sight of the ait and the lazy blue threads of water around the sandbars.

My father said, "What pigs?"

"The old sow and her pigs," I said, surprised. "The time the river flooded. I remember how the water rose right up to their feet."

My father said, "The Judith never got that high, and there never was any pigs up there."

"Yes there were! I remember!" I could see the little pigs as clearly as I could see my father, and I could remember exactly how my own skin had shriveled as they cringed back from the water and butted the sow for cold comfort.

My father shook his head. "How did you think pigs would get up there?" he asked.

Of course they couldn't.

His logic settled on me like an awakening in ordinary daylight. Of course a sow could not lead nine or ten suckling pigs up those sheer fifteen-foot crumbling dirt sides, even for fear of their lives. And why, after all, would pigs even try to scramble to the top of such a precarious perch when they could escape a cloudburst by following any one of the cattle trails or deer trails that webbed the cutbanks on both sides of the river?

Had there been a cloudburst at all? Had there been pigs?

No, my father repeated. The Judith had never flooded anywhere near that high in our time. Bill Hafer had always raised a few pigs when we lived down there on the river, but he kept them penned up. No.

| | | | | | |

Today I lean on the open window of my car and yawn and listen to the sounds of late summer. The snapping of grasshoppers. Another car approaching on the highway, roaring past my shoulder of the road, then fading away until I can hear the faint scratches of some small hidden creature in the weeds. I am bone-deep in landscape. In this dome of sky and river and undeflected sunlight, in this illusion of timelessness, I can almost feel my body, blood, and breath in the broken line of the bluffs and the pervasive scent of ripening sweet clover and dust, almost feel the sagging fence line of ancient cedar posts stapled across my vitals.

The only shade in sight is across the river where box elders lean over a low white frame house with a big modern house trailer parked behind it. Downstream, far away, a man works along a ditch. I think he might be the husband of a second cousin of mine who still lives on her old family place. My cousins wouldn't know me if they stopped and asked me what I was doing here.

Across the highway, a trace of a road leads through a barbed-wire gate and sharply up the bluff. It is the old cutoff to Danvers, a town that has dried up and blown away. I have heard that the cutoff has washed out, further up the river, but down here it still holds a little bleached gravel. Almost as though my father might turn off in his battered truck at fifteen miles an hour, careful of his bald wartime tires, while I lie on the seat with my head on his thigh and take my nap. Almost as though at the end of that road will be the two grain elevators pointing sharply out of the hazy olives and ochers of the grass into the rolling cumulus, and two or three graveled streets with traffic moving past the pool hall and post office and dug-out store where, when I wake from my nap and scramble down from the high seat of the truck, Old Man Longin will be waiting behind his single glass display case with my precious wartime candy bar.

Yes, that little girl was me, I guess. A three-year-old standing on the unswept board floor, looking up at rows of canned goods on shelves that were nailed against the logs in the 1880s, when Montana was still a territory. The dust smelled the same to her as it does to me now.

Across the river, that low white frame house where my cousin still lives is the old Sample place. Ninety years ago a man named Sample fell in love with a woman named Carrie. Further up the bottom—you can't see it from here because of the cottonwoods—stands Carrie's deserted house in what used to be a fenced yard. Forty years ago Carrie's house was full of three generations of her family, and the yard was full of cousins at play. Sixty years ago the young man who would be my father rode on horseback down that long hill to Carrie's house, and Sample said to Carrie, *Did your brother Albert ever have a son? From the way the kid sits his horse, he must be your brother's son.*

Or so the story goes. Sample was murdered. Carrie died in her sleep. My father died of exposure.

| | | | | | |

The Judith winds toward its mouth. Its current seems hardly
to move. Seeing it in August, so blue and unhurried, it is
difficult to believe how many drownings or near drownings
the Judith has counted over the years. To a stranger it surely
must look insignificant, hardly worth calling a river.

In 1805 the explorers Lewis and Clark, pausing in their
quest for the Pacific, saw the mountains and the prairies of
central Montana and the wild game beyond reckoning. They
also noted this river, which they named after a girl. Lewis
and Clark were the first white recorders of this place. In
recording it, they altered it. However indifferent to the his-
torical record, those who see this river and hear its name,
Judith, see it in a slightly different way because Lewis and
Clark saw it and wrote about it.

In naming the river, Lewis and Clark claimed it for a system
of governance that required a wrenching of the fundamental
connections between landscape and its inhabitants. This particular drab sagebrush pocket of the West was never, perhaps,
holy ground. None of the landmarks here is invested with
the significance of the sacred buttes to the north. For the
Indian tribes that hunted here, central Montana must have
been commonplace, a familiar stretch of their lives, a place
to ride and breathe and be alive.

But even this drab pocket is now a part of the history of
the West, which, through a hundred and fifty years of white
settlement and economic development, of rapid depletion of
water and coal and timber and topsoil, of dependence upon
military escalation and federal subsidies, has been a history
of the transformation of landscape from a place to be alive
in into a place to own. This is a transformation that breaks
connections, that holds little in common. My deepest associations with this sunlit river are private. Without a connection between outer and inner landscape, I cannot tell my

father what I saw. "There never was a sow in the river," he said, embarrassed at my notion. And yet I know there was a sow in the river.

| | | | | | |

All who come and go bring along their own context, leave their mark, however faint. If the driver glanced out the window of that car that just roared past, what did he see? Tidy irrigated alfalfa fields, a small green respite from the dryland miles? That foreshortened man who works along the ditch, does he straighten his back from his labors and see his debts spread out in irrigation pipes and electric pumps?

It occurs to me that I dreamed the sow in the river at a time when I was too young to sort out dreams from daylight reality or to question why they should be sorted out and dismissed. As I think about it, the episode does contain some of the characteristics of a dream. That futile, endless, convoluted search in the rain, for example. The absence of sound in the cab of the truck, and the paralysis of the onlookers on the brink of that churning current. For now that I know she never existed outside my imagination, I think I do recognize that sow on her slippery pinnacle.

Memory lights upon a dream as readily as an external event, upon a set of rusty irrigation pipes and a historian's carefully detailed context through which she recalls the collective memory of the past. As memory saves, discards, retrieves, fails to retrieve, its logic may well be analogous to the river's inexorable search for the lowest ground. The trivial and the profound roll like leaves to the surface. Every ripple is suspect.

Today the Judith River spreads out in the full sunlight of August, oblivious of me and my precious associations, indifferent to the emotional context I have framed it with. My memory seems less a record of landscape and event than a superimposition upon what otherwise would continue to flow, leaf out, or crumble according to its lot. What I remember is far less trustworthy than the story I tell about it. The possibility for connection lies in story.

Whether or not I dreamed her, the sow in the river is my story. She is what I have saved, up there on her pinnacle where the river roils.

READING
ABRAHAM

Abraham and Mary Hogeland, 1890.

| | | | | | | | | | | | | | | | | | | | | | | | | | | | | | | | | | | | | | | | | |

*A*s far back as I can remember, a framed photograph of my great-grandparents hung in the house where I grew up. She had died long before I was born, and he a year or two after I was born. As a child I thought they were profoundly uninteresting. I knew their names—Abraham and Mary Walton Hogeland—and I knew that, in 1882, when Montana was still a territory, they had established a ranch and raised a large family on the very ground where I played among the willows along Spring Creek and tried to imagine my way past the river bluffs.

My great-aunts and uncles told stories in which their gray-haired selves were transformed back into the hell-raising boys and girls they had been, or believed they had been, on the turn-of-the-century Montana frontier. It seemed to me that the willows and creek had been full of children in those days, reverberating with shouts and laughter I had been born too late to hear. They were the stars of their own stories, the hell-raisers, while their parents, Abraham and Mary, so adult that their faces were dressed stone, receded into a single dimension of authority to be plotted against and outwitted. To me, listening to the stories, Abraham and Mary were never flesh and blood.

Later I came to disapprove of Abraham and to believe that he would have disapproved of me. Abraham had been a paterfamilias, an oppressor, a traditionalist like my father, who had tried to keep me home on the ranch; and I had left Montana by then and begun work on a Ph.D., and I was smarting from the barbs and obstacles that had been flung in my way.

Then, while I was still in my twenties, still in graduate school, my grandmother gave me a bundle of Abraham's papers that she had been trying to read.

It was an odd assortment of scrap paper, flattened old envelopes and pages torn from pocket ledgers, closely written in pencil and tied in string. My grandmother never told me how she had come by them, or why she had so carefully preserved such inconsequential stuff. I untied the bundle and made an attempt at transcribing one or two pages, but I found Abraham's writing indecipherable, and not just because of his blurred pencil script. These were descriptions of nature, from what I could make out, purple passages, repetitive, embarrassing, clotted with words like *infinite* and *reverential*.

Still, I took Abraham's papers, telling my grandmother I would try someday to read them. I put them away in a chest. My grandmother never mentioned them again. She had already begun her slow killing spiral into senility. She rummaged through her trunk of memorabilia and papers, reading as though for the first time the letters written to her by her husband, Abraham's son, dead fifty years. Then she took her scissors to them. They were hers; no one stopped her. But as those snips and filigrees of yellowed paper fell into patternless clutter, I felt the illicit, surviving bundle I had hidden like a heartbeat in the till of my chest.

Abraham's papers became my sole knowledge as the generation who would have known or cared about them died.

Although I never untied the string or tried to read the fine scrawl again, occasionally I looked to be sure they were still in the till, or touched them: a fading collection in pencil on the softening envelopes and backs of official correspondence and unused letterhead from the Office of the Fergus County Surveyor, a bundle that would have fit into a shoe box. It was gradually disintegrating into a wad.

| | | | | | |

The years following my father's death were harrowed by further losses. Drought and a depressed agricultural economy had eroded Montana's tax base and drained the state's support of its institutions, and Northern Montana College, which had been a part of me for so long, could no longer afford me.

"Institutions thrive on people like you," a friend had warned me. "Institutions take and take and take, but they can't give anything back."

Sometimes at night I lay awake listening to the wind ripping off the birch leaves outside my window and heard my father's words, like an unwanted legacy, censorious, deluded, deaf to any answer: *Somewhere you got the idea in your head that you know something, but you don't know a goddamned thing.*

| | | | | | |

I felt as ragged as the birch leaves, but I had a child to support. By 1987, I had left Montana and moved to Idaho, on the confluence of the Clearwater and Snake rivers, where the narrow gorge of the Lolo Pass spreads out beyond the soft hills of the Palouse and the Camas Prairie into the bare gray bluffs of the westward-seeking Columbia. With the Continental Divide at my back, a buffer against the high plains that had claimed half my life, I settled into this new terrain with my daughter. I was teaching again, a little awkwardly after years in higher ed administration, and finding time to write.

Then, at Christmas, I opened the envelope from my sister and took out the print of my great-grandparents' photograph and looked at a face as familiar as my own pulse: a man whose handsome arched brows and eyes, forever fixed beyond me into the middle distance, were my father's to the life. Haunted, I sat and studied the fine lines, the familiar mouth and cheekbones, the austere shape of the head.

How could I not have seen that resemblance until now? The sudden, uncanny revelation of the arrangements of genes that, passing through the generations like a time capsule exploding across one set of features and missing another, accounted for the likeness between Abraham and my father? In many ways Abraham's photograph was a better likeness of my father than any I possessed. Always private, my father had never allowed a studio photograph to be taken of him, and in snapshots his face invariably was cast in shadow.

But not Abraham, who turns three-quarter-face to the photographer with an ease my father never showed. His wife, Mary, stands behind him looking stalwart, but Abraham leans back in the ornate armchair of a nineteenth-century studio. He has crossed one knee over the other. His left hand lies casually on his thigh; his right hand rests in the pocket of his dark worsted suit trousers. Though his accoutrements are those of the paterfamilias—the mustache, the formal clothes, the watch chain across the vest—his posture exudes an easy energy, a humor that contradicts the formality. Those are laugh lines around his eyes. Under the mustache, Abraham is enjoying himself.

Studying that disturbing likeness—my father, yet not my father—I felt rising anger and resolve. By God, Abraham, *he* may have left me without saying goodbye, but *you*, Abraham! I know how to make you talk to me!

I went to my chest and lifted out the bundle of Abraham's papers, and felt the dust of nearly a century stick to my fingers. The pencil scrawl had been nearly illegible when I first tried to read it. Would it be faded beyond recovery by now?

I marched downstairs, cradling the pound of ancient, flaking paper in my two hands, and laid the bundle gently on my desk beside the computer. I turned on a high-intensity lamp and got a magnifying glass.

Untying the string and gently picking loose the first folded ivory paper from the top of the stack, my hands trembled.

Before me was a legal-sized envelope that had been cut open with scissors, flattened, and refolded. One side was addressed to *Abraham Hogeland* in spidery brown ink and postmarked November 28, 6 P.M., 1902. The other side was covered with the minuscule pencil script I remembered, and my heart sank. It was too late; too many years had passed; a blur was all that was left. And some of the papers deeper in the stack were worse. Some were so faded as to be hardly recognizable as handwriting, let alone decipherable. And where was Abraham's starting point on the envelope in front of me? Where was his ending?

Sitting there in the circle of lamplight with the hum of the computer and the glow of its screen, I studied my great-grandfather's handwriting and saw a word swim up.

The shimmering light—falling?— No, that mark is a caret. He has written between the lines. And his next few words are scribbled over the embossed reverse side of the postmark. I can't make them out. Never mind, push ahead. You can always come back to it.

—through clefts in the— No, this is impossible, and the embossed spot is coming up again. Never mind. Key in question marks for the words you cannot read and go on.

—grotesque by—portrait?— That doesn't make sense. *????
???? flooding the snow clad meadows.*

Suddenly, a complete line of clarity. *Then the flood of moon
light falling on the dark running waters of Spring Creek—*

Like a touchstone, the name rang over the years: Spring
Creek, the trout stream that rises from the Big Springs of
central Montana and winds through the old home ranch on
its way to the Judith River. My breath caught. Abraham, I
know within a mile or two of where you are writing!

Days later I had rendered the complete passage. The magnifying glass turned out to be an annoyance, as it further
blurred and distorted the already faint clues. But holding his
papers under my lamp, I read faster as I became acquainted
with Abraham's idiosyncratic *e*'s and *r*'s, the flourishes on
his *p*'s, and the hasty way the crosses of his *t*'s fell an inch
further along the line than the letter itself. *Portrait* turned
out to be *contrast*. A single unbroken waver with a *d* on the
end, I came to be certain from its context, was *emerald*.

The shimmering light of the full moon as it rises over
the hill falling here and there through clefts in the rocks
makes the shadows on the snow clad road seem grotesque by contrast with the pure calm light flooding the
snow clad meadows.

Then the flood of moon light falling on the dark running waters of Spring Creek to silver the crest of each
ripple while the troughs are of emerald or of deep blue.

The rhythmic hoof beats of my horses echo & re echo
from the over hanging cliffs, my buggy wheels singing
constantly drone a monotonous chant to old King Frost.
The large cottonwoods in freezing pop now & then almost as loud as the report of a pistol shot. We know
without seeing a thermometer that the night is very cold.

Now that I had it captured on the screen of my word processor, I studied this passage. Heavily participial, unintentionally repetitious, weighted with the conventional personification, my great-grandfather's style was as embarrassingly self-conscious as I had remembered it. All the reasons why that condescending young graduate student, his great-granddaughter, had abandoned Abraham's papers in the first place were glowing on the screen in front of me.

What pulled me out of my embarrassment now was Abraham's exact sense of time and place. I was pretty sure I knew almost to the mile where Abraham had sat in his buggy on a winter night in late 1902 or early 1903. I knew about the snowfields on both sides of the dark running water, and about the bluffs ("over hanging cliffs"), and the clear thirty-below-zero night. I knew where to find his road, and these things I knew not so much spatially, geographically, as internally, as I might slowly recognize a map of my own arteries. Abraham had seen the bluffs and running water of my childhood, of my father's childhood, and, in the act of writing about them, had told me he saw what I saw in a way that transcended style. Surely, if I kept transcribing, I might learn something about the magnet pull of place, perhaps even how to break it.

I tried to remember everything I ever had heard about Abraham. I knew he had been born in Bucks County, Pennsylvania, in 1855, and that he had attended Lafayette College. He had become a surveyor for the Northern Pacific Railroad. In 1882 he came to the Montana Territory with the railroad, but left it to start a ranch at the mouth of Spring Creek in Fergus County. For a number of years he had been the Fergus County surveyor. My high school geometry teacher had known him. He described for me how, in the early days, the plats were measured by the revolutions of a buggy wheel. Abraham's buggy had covered every mile of central Montana. As a teenager my father had driven with him to carry his chains and had picked up the rudiments of surveying from him.

Surveying is the application of geometry and trigonometry to achieve a representation of the land on a reduced scale. Surveying exchanges one perspective for another; it exchanges the physical for the abstract. As land is measured, it shrinks into its dollar equivalent. It can be purchased or sold. With its conversion into capital, land loses its primacy; it becomes a resource. Part of this process in Montana in the waning years of the nineteenth century was the conversion of land from a place where the Blackfeet, Assiniboine, Crow, and other northern plains tribes lived into sections and half- and quarter-sections that white settlers owned.

It was Abraham's task to transform a thousand square miles of primeval grassland into straight lines and right angles on a map, to convert landscape into property. With his level and transit, rods and chains, Abraham measured the benches, creek and river bottoms, hills, coulees, and low mountains of central Montana into accurate boundaries for homesteads. In the process, he tried to describe what he saw on the scrap paper he carried in his pockets.

Just what Abraham saw was, for me, an insistent unknown. For several weeks I read his notes compulsively in my quest to recover his vision. I pored over the minuscule script on the backs of receipts and the insides of envelopes, searching for clues to dates, circumstances, intentions. I stole time for him. Hours passed while I huddled over his carets and crossings-out in the circle of lamplight on the lower floor of my house, absorbed, guessing, pausing to key into my computer what at last I could understand. Long after midnight I would be promising myself, like an addict, just one more sentence. I filled a diskette, started another, and found that his disturbed papers had left a thin film of ancient dust on my IBM.

After all those hours alone with his notes in the lamplight, becoming so familiar with his crabbed, impatient handwriting that I would have recognized it if a letter from him arrived in my mailbox, learning to predict the loose clauses of his grammar, the hasty absence of punctuation, the characteristic recurrence of certain adjectives, I began to feel an intimacy like the first unspoiled stages of a love affair. As I lifted the sense from that hundred-year-old pencil scrawl and transferred it to the screen of the word processor, I could hardly believe that an experience so intense could be entirely one-sided. Gradually the conviction sank in that I was the only person ever to have read most of these notes.

| | | | | | |

As I got better at reading his handwriting, I began to remember stories with clues about Abraham as faint as his crossings-out and compulsive revisions. One afternoon my daughter and her best friend ran in from school and flung themselves upside down in a chair in my workroom. As the little girls giggled and waved their legs in the air, putting an end to my work, I remembered an anecdote a cousin had told me. In his latter years Abraham had been a justice of the peace. One New Year's Day, with his family gathered for the holiday dinner, a young couple had come to his house to be married. While Abraham performed the ceremony, his grandchildren shrieked and slid down the banister and chased each other back up the stairs to slide down again. "We made such a racket," said my cousin, "that the couple could hardly hear themselves getting married."

Was he patient with children? Or merely too removed from them to be annoyed? Was I to believe the best or the worst about this man who had shaped my life without ever bestowing a word or perhaps even a glance at me?

| | | | | | |

Reading Abraham, in the beginning, was learning to beware of my own expectations. In the following passage I supposed at first that, like an on-the-scene reporter of local color, he was describing a day in the life of the bullwhackers who drove the big freight wagons from Lewistown to Fort Benton:

At the top of the Arrow Creek Hill (a hill which the freighters always declare "hangs over a little") as one of the off bronchos could not be brought back into the road with the whip Frenchy took the tongue at a leap but just as he struck the ground an especially obstreperous broncho on the off wheel kicked him. . . . We ran up to help Frenchy but he was insensible and continued in that state for twenty four hours.

The road is very narrow, and in many places a grade is made around cut banks 175 ft. high.

Fortunately the road was clear ahead and away they went. We watched the wild run.

You have played crack the whip.

At every turn, the trail wagon was the popper but it righted and right side up with care again it went on . . . the leaders were a good lively yoke and thoroughly broke to keep the road but several times a miss step made by one of the string on the narrow grade looked as if we would have a surplus of coyote bait & kindling wood.

Is this passage a kind of diary entry on scratch paper? Or does the implied reader ("You have played crack the whip") suggest that Abraham was making notes for a letter or essay? I am particularly struck by what it omits. For a man who took pains in describing moonlight and snow and running water, Abraham is curiously terse here. No detailed descriptions of the bull teams or their drivers or freight, no attempt at preserving this moment of the vanishing frontier. Abraham must know that the bull teams soon will be made obsolete by the railroads he helped bring to Montana, but he is not nostalgic about them. He wants to get on with his narrative.

What, then?

I have driven down the Arrow Creek Hill by night and day, over black ice in winter and scabs of ruptured gravel and asphalt in summer, and while the road has been paved for years, it still is narrow, and its grades wind over cutbanks as deep and sheer as Abraham said they were. To imagine a freight wagon "popping" down that grade at the end of a string of runaway bulls is enough to bring me up out of Abraham's text and set me right beside him as, over Frenchy's senseless body, he watches "the wild run."

And I am struck by the kinds of things Abraham knows about, the day-to-day details of the frontier that must have been hard-learned by the young graduate of Lafayette College. When Frenchy, for example, seeing that his team was out of control, "took the tongue at a leap," he was following a rule of teamsters that probably descends from the Roman charioteers and certainly saved the life of an aunt of mine when a team of horses ran away with her and a mowing machine: *In a runaway, always jump for the tongue and hang on.*

But who was Frenchy?

Could he have been the shadowy Frenchy Pernot who turned up in some of my father's stories? I have in my files a newspaper article, written by one of their old neighbors in connection with the Montana centennial celebration, about Abraham and his brother Theo. It reads in part:

> Sheep were sheared once a year with hand shears. . . .
> Each fleece was tied with string and tramped into large

bags, 3′ × 12′. These were hauled to Fort Benton with oxen, later with horses.

One man doing this was Frenchy Pernot.

Were Abraham and his brother hauling fleeces to Fort Benton when they had a runaway on the Arrow Creek Hill? Was it his year's income Abraham watched on its hell-bent descent down that road? If this is the case, his narrative takes a different shape from the local-color reporting I first thought I was reading. In telling of an event as trivial, after a hundred years, as the dust it briefly raised, as trivial as the identity of Frenchy Pernot, Abraham's narrative becomes personal, a revelation of self in the not-quite-lost moment. What matters, finally, in this passage, is that on an uncertain hour, day, year (the only clue here is that he was writing on a grocer's receipt headed *Lewistown, Montana, 189__*) Abraham snatched paper and pencil from his pocket and saved that moment.

Why? Why did Abraham write?

I ask the question again and again, and, as I read the whole of his papers, find no single answer. The bundle contains, for instance, several versions of what appears to be a short story about two young boys trailing horse thieves. Notes on the economics of sheep raising I think may be drafts for political speeches or for letters to newspapers. One thick packet in violet pencil turns out, disappointingly, to be remedies for diseases in chickens.

But Abraham also copied out excerpts from Shakespeare, Pope, Cowper, Byron (and, for God's sake, Joanna Baillie, who wrote verse dramas about passion in the late eighteenth and early nineteenth centuries. What kind of curriculum did they have at Lafayette College? I've never known anyone who has read a line of Joanna Baillie.). And lists of staples and reckonings of mileage and surveying notes are written in the margins of much revised poems of his own. The stained, fragmented paper suggests that he wrote quickly on whatever he had at hand, perhaps in the course of some of those endless miles in his buggy. Again and again I find fragments, like the description of Spring Creek in winter or the runaway freight team on the Arrow Creek Hill, that have the spontaneous tone of a eyewitness saving what he saw.

Was Abraham writing only for himself on those odds and ends of papers? If what he was keeping was a kind of fragmented diary, why did he revise so carefully, why did he strain for a literary tone? Why did he so carefully preserve the scraps?

The one common thread I find in Abraham's papers is the sense that he is recounting his adventures in the Montana Territory to someone who has never seen a runaway bull team or heard cottonwoods pop on a freezing night. An unparticularized someone, perhaps back in civilized, stately Pennsylvania. His narrative has to do with how he sees himself, A. Hogeland of Bucks County, honors graduate of one of the most prestigious Presbyterian colleges in America, as he kneels in the alkali dust at the side of poor senseless, anonymous Frenchy and watches his bull team stampeding down the raw frontier grade. What a sight! What a story! Abraham's face is alight with the irony, the humor of it. He is itching for the slip of paper and pencil stub even before the wagon loaded with his fleeces, still miraculously right side up, rattles to a stop and settles back on four wheels behind the heaving bulls in a cloud of dust at the bottom of the Arrow Creek Hill.

Abraham is at his most self-aware when he is most conscious that he stands a little apart from what he observes:

> The tinkling of the sheep bells, an occasional bark of a dog or a dull bleat of a sheep as she hurriedly goes from one isolated bunch of grass to another, were the only sounds breaking the solitude.

The sobbing of the gusty wind in the scattering pine trees emphasized the dreary picture of jutting sandstone ledges in an expanse of sage brush covered bad lands. . . . The sheep corraled, then into a dreary cabin, with cottonwood and an open fireplace to get supper.

With tears streaming down my cheeks I at last sit down to a supper of potatoes, bacon, burnt flap jacks and smoked coffee.

Away back in Pennsylvania a little wife is singing a lullaby to a baby born but a few days before I came west to build a ranchhouse.

For this stranger in a strange desolate land, the cure for homesickness was to transform the wasteland into something more to his liking. For Abraham, one means of transformation was economic. His notes abound with percentages and profit margins, with theories on the practicability of sheep ranching in the Judith Basin country he continually praises for its resources: its fresh water, its sheltering timber, its winter grazing.

Abraham discovered that writing about the northern plains was another means of transforming them into space he could measure and control. The draft of his short story shows he was aware of the conventional Western of his day and the ways in which its melodramatic plot line defines perspective. The forays of his stereotypical scout against stereotypical outlaws seem oddly juxtaposed against an actual landscape that I can locate today. Perhaps Abraham himself was aware of the distance between the West as romantic invention and the West as he knew it, for it is on his description of the real landscape that he lavishes the most care. Though he nearly drives me crazy when he comes to the bottom of his inside-out envelope and breaks off just as he reaches the crux of his narrative, I think some of his most zestful prose springs from his fly fishing for rainbow trout in a stream that one day will be nationally famous:

> . . . in that deepest blue spot just where you see that big rush of the under tow as it rolls to the top and turns a summersault is where I hooked the big trout last week.

> Just between the summit and the swirl I dropped my fly and let it float I had floated to the end of my line and just as I started to raise the pole he took the bait.

> The reel fairly hissed. I attempted to check him with the brake then with the pole but I soon found I had a fighter.

> I drew down on him all I dared but knew if I landed him I would have to run for it.

> See that drift log by the wire fence I was over the fence the next step after I struck that log.

> He was at the end of the line just as I made the raise and I tightened up to catch my balance. . . .

Family legend confirms his love for the basin—how he first surveyed it for the railroad and, having seen no better country between Pennsylvania and Montana, decided to make it his. He filed homestead papers on a sheltered valley at the mouth of Spring Creek and built the cabin on the slope where his next seven children were born. (The "little wife" brought his first child, the baby born but a few days before he left for the West, out to Montana the next year, and Abraham could stop burning his own flapjacks over a fire of wet cottonwood logs.)

Abraham wrote very little about his family or about his feelings beyond conventional sentiment. The stories I heard as a child tell me more, though their margins are as blurred as his handwriting: Abraham, unruffled, performing that wedding ceremony amidst the din of grandchildren. Abraham, when his wife went into labor in the cabin on the slope, sending three-year-old Albert to ride three miles on horseback to bring back a neighbor woman to assist with his sister Carrie's birth.

"There I was, all alone," Abraham told my aunt, who told me, "I wanted to say, 'Bah! *You* were all alone?'"

The part of that story that fascinated me when I heard it as a child was how Albert had ridden the three miles alone. The road he took was the one I later followed to school, and many afternoons I have dawdled and tried to see the little boy on his horse, hanging on to the mane as they climbed the steep shale hill, then followed the fence line across the flats, past the rotted pile of logs that had been that very Aunt Carrie's own homestead cabin, years later—but the little boy! What had he done when he got to the wire gate, which I, at seven, couldn't open?

Perhaps there hadn't been a wire gate in those days. For although much remained of Abraham's homestead, much more had changed by the time I could remember it. Two hills over from our ranch buildings lay a weedy stretch that Grammy called the Sheepshed Bottom. Years later I saw a damaged photograph, like an alternate reality, of the Bottom in the days of Abraham's sheepsheds and all his jugs and pens, his barns and corrals.

And yet I hardly wondered what they were really like, those grandparents whose lives along the creek bottom had shaped the meadows like palm prints and worn the ruts in the road. A land surveyor and a woman who cherished trees. Our landmarks carried the names they had given them: Theo's Butte, the Box Canyon, the Water Coulee. Where I rode my pony, he had herded his sheep and she had gathered dry twigs—squaw wood—for a hot fire to bake biscuits for her children.

The two-story log house Abraham later built still stood in my childhood with its back to the creek and its blank windows facing the bluffs. Soft gray curls lifted from its logs, and hollyhocks and phlox planted by my great-grandmother poked through murdock and Canadian thistle, and her cottonwoods, grown to decayed giants, shed their bark and trash around the door. We children were forbidden to play there, but my mother and Grammy let us come along when they went to retrieve some of the fruit jars or plates they had stored in the old kitchen.

"Stay out of the weeds!" they warned. "There might be rattlesnakes!"

A china doorknob opened into the thickened odor of motionless air and decay, and mouse droppings littered the floorboards and crunched underfoot. A stair rose in the gloom, and on either hand was a door. The one on the left opened into the old kitchen. Its walls had once been plastered, and a cleanish oblong lay in the middle of the floor, as though linoleum had been taken up. Phlox looked in through the boards on the windows. Beyond the back door was a ten-foot drop to the creek.

"One time when your dad was a little boy, he rode his wagon right out that door," Grammy warned us. My father had been born in June of 1913 in one of those airless upstairs bedrooms.

While I knew my great-grandmother had still been living in the homestead cabin in June of 1889 when a man in a wagon stopped and asked her the way to the river, I always imagined it was on the road outside these windows that she heard the oversized wheels rumble to a stop and went out to see the looming canvas top and the man on the wagon seat who shouted his question without climbing down. He had nine dead bodies under that canvas cover, as it turned out, and he drove a few miles farther, down to Sample's Crossing, and buried them in a gravel bar.

I studied an 1889 newspaper article and learned that there were five dead bodies, not nine. Several witnesses told the coroner's jury they had seen the man and the wagon and had their suspicions, but my great-grandmother was not one of them.

"—*he wouldn't tell where he was going, which was suspicious in itself in those days. Grandma said a neighbor had stopped by the cabin that day, and he was so curious about that wagon that he put his foot up on the wheel, as if to look inside. Grandma said if he had, she supposed he and she and all the children would have been under that canvas with the others.*"

The writer for the Fergus County *Argus* took a more righteous tone than my great-grandmother's, but he clearly shared my love for detail:

The murderer's final deed was in perfect keeping with the demon he has shown himself to be by his life's conduct. No one but a fiend incarnate could have conceived and carried out such a means for self-destruction. Tearing a wide strip off the blanket on his bed he tied it for a loop in the top of his cell. For a hangman's rope he tore a slip off the pillowslip made of new and heavy cotton. Taking his silk handkerchief he tied his right arm and ankle together. He then slipped his head into the prepared noose, his body all the time reclining on his couch. He made a slip knot into which he put his left ankle and fastened his left wrist to the ankle. Both feet being thus drawn up so that they would not touch the floor when he fell, he rolled himself off the bed and in a moment was a dangling corpse.

As for the victims:

> . . . they were consigned to their untimely, final resting place by strangers with care and kindliness. But yesterday, as it were, buoyant with health and bright hopes, today they sleep on the banks of the Judith river, slain by the hands of a demon in human form whom the dead had succored.

The photograph of the dead at Sample's Crossing is too damaged for details. I think the bluff in the background is the site of the present Judith River bridge. The gravel bar is within sight of the highway today. In the photograph it has been laid open in two deep trenches. Six blurry individuals, one of them with a dog at his heels, a few of them holding some kind of implements, are standing around the exhumed bodies. Behind them are the cowboys who found the bodies while they were driving cattle through the crossing. Eleven of them, on horseback, lined up in a careful pose for posterity.

The newspaper writer added a detail Grammy never mentioned. "The coroner's jury, impanelled and sworn to examine into the cause of death of the five bodies lying before them, consisted of A. Hogeland, foreman . . ."

Had Abraham's close involvement seemed less compelling to Grammy than his wife's narrow escape? Or did she simply know her story more intimately than his? And why was Grammy's story (and, presumably, my great-grandmother's) one of fortunate disengagement, compared with the macabre fascination of the *Argus* article?

| | | | | | |

Abraham controlled the space that stretched beyond his imagination by measuring and mapping it for settlement. As he wrote about that external world he was pinning down and mapping and limiting, he seems not to have been aware how much he was concealing in the telling, or how much, in the process of his mapping, he was erasing of a landscape and a way of living.

A much creased and water-stained fragment from the bottom of the bundle of papers tells what A. Hogeland of Bucks County saw (and failed to see) through the telescope on his surveyor's transit:

That was "a great josh" of Nortons on that bunch of Jockos the other day said Hal . . .

Oh! I heard Wheeler trying to tell it but he laughed so much that I soon was disgusted & quit.

Norton Wheeler & I, said Hal, were down below the mouth of the canyon changing that compound curve to two simple one of ten degrees, quite a slow tedious piece of work, especially as it threw the line further up in the old placer working. While we were at work a bunch of Jockos came along and camped just below us. Their horses were turned out on the side hill opposite to us. After dinner as we had worked down near them the "bucks" came over to us and Norton soon had them squinting through the telescope of the transit.

One fellow, evidently the leader, was given first "shoot" and when he saw that the trees, rocks &t were drawn apparently so close he gave forth a pleased Ugh! Ugh! Ugh! and made an up & down motion with his hand at the end of the telescope to show that the object was right there. The same pantomime was gone through with by the balance of them, but one young buck to show he was not interested by such childs play went off some ten or fifteen yards seating himself on a knoll which happened to be toward the horses.

Norton flanged the telescope and turned it end for end and pointed it towards the fellow on the knoll and called up the leader, who took a peep. The young fellow on the knoll appeared away off, seemingly near the horses.

Here the paper has flaked away from the top of the grocer's receipt Abraham is writing on, destroying several lines which probably describe the Indian's surprise in seeing his friend so reduced in size. I want to scold him before I read further— *Abraham, you're embarrassing me with your "bucks" and your ugh, ugh, ughs! Abraham, can't you see the reductiveness of tunnel vision?*
But Hal resumes his story:

The others went through the same performance. By George, Abe, the way those injums looked holes in that side hill was a caution. They talked "injum" and they talked signs "heap good."

Just then the leader came back to take another look and Norton motioned to our friend on the knoll to come to him.

He arose while the leader was looking and then the jabbering & the signs took a good natured turn. They all crowded around each explaining to the other how the thing happened but they would not touch anything nor attempt to look through the telescope without being asked, though they made their wishes very evident by their looks.

Abraham then editorializes (and reveals, through his inadvertent syntax, the psychological side of converting Indian land into white settlement):

> The Jockos are a peace loving tribe of the flathead country where the agents have been very successful in civilizing and learning agriculture. When east of the main range of the Rockies hunting or selling horns they are very much afraid of the Piegans & Crows.

I felt stale and saddened as I came to the end of Abraham's papers. His vision, like my father's, was linear; it ruled out the faces on the margins or at the shrunken end of his perspective, and one of those faces was mine.

Where could I find certain footing or even air to breathe in his world of right angles? Seen through Abraham's tunnel vision, I was a runaway daughter, a failed "little wife," an uppity woman who *somehow got the idea in her head she knows something, but by God she don't know a goddamned thing.* Within the terms of Abraham's conversion of place from habitat to real estate, with all its concurrent assumptions about patriarchy and patrimony, I was left with no more integrity of self than the Jockos.

I had brought Abraham to life, but his life and mine seemed mutually exclusive. As I had suspected from the beginning, Abraham and I had nothing to say to one another and no way to say it if we did.

In the spring of 1990 I went back to Montana, to Great Falls, where I spoke to the Friends of the Public Library about my fascination and disquietude with Abraham and his papers. An old friend from Northern Montana College, himself a great-grandson of plains settlers, listened from the audience. He was intrigued, he said, by the apparent contradiction of Abraham's choice of medium—his scrap paper—and his careful preservation of such ephemeral texts. A day or two later I got a long letter from him.

"I feel compelled to think he had some rather specific audience in mind," my friend wrote. "It struck me at an early hour this morning, in a hazy vision of Abraham stopping by Spring Creek, that undoubtedly he had you in mind all the time as audience—or the persona of you that we all carry with us when we speculate about our descendants unknown and their view of us. I think perhaps Abraham had you specifically in mind as audience, and what a touching and lonely act his writing then becomes."

| | | | | | | |

Abraham, in my imagination your buggy rolls over the prairie swells toward the bristling fringe of pines along the river breaks. On the horizon is the blue line of the butte your son's artist friend, a self-taught kid named Russell who ran away from St. Louis to become a cowboy, loved to paint into the background of his scenes of the Old West. Russell found a way to contain what he saw in oils. But you, Abraham, in your suit and vest and watch chain, you hold the reins. Your horses break into a trot, and you brace yourself on the footboard and lean into the wind, still zestful, still as lean and limber as a young man, although your shreds of hair are white now. The towheaded boy in the back seat, your grandson, bumps against your folded transit and chains and the fishing tackle you carry everywhere you go. He wonders how long he will have to wait if you decide to stop and go fishing this afternoon. He is a good boy, careful and accurate like you. Like you, he can add a column of numbers in his head faster than a clerk in a bank can use a calculating machine. He learns quickly, but he has inherited your talent without your opportunities; there will be no Lafayette College for this boy growing up in the West. And he has grown up with your love for the Judith Basin without your long vision; only three times in his life will he venture far from the shadow of that blue butte.

Abraham, your photograph hangs over my desk. Above the reflection on the glass from the window opposite, Mary stands stalwart behind you while your gaze is set eternally over my shoulder. In the reflection, superimposed over you and Mary in your good formal dark clothes, the Snake River spreads its slow current as it rolls toward its confluence. The early lights of winter glow on the far bank of the Snake and glow again in the reflected depths of your photograph. I am a long way from home.

Abraham, weren't you struck by the astonishment of those Indians who saw their world suddenly reduced through the telescope of the surveyor's transit that day? Didn't you wonder what they said to each other when, with the casual flip of a glass, the surveyor suddenly altered their vision from a dizzying close focus on rocks and trees to a glimpse of one of their number in miniature at the end of a tunnel? Who missed the point of the joke that day, Abraham?

Your papers rest on my desk, soft and limp and yellow, numbered in my careful ink, their contents filed on diskettes. They still retain something of their old potency, though I don't know how long it will last. I am afraid they are disintegrating. Their surfaces are like moulting velvet under my fingertips, although the lines upon tiny lines of soft pencil script now are almost as recognizable as faces. Words, words, words, more words, the shapes for what we otherwise would never know, the stuff by which we reduce the terror of endlessness, as you, Abraham, understood so well.

DIRT
ROADS

Left to right: Mary, Betty, Doris, Jack, 1947.

|||||||||||||||||||||||||||||||||||||||||||||||||

*O*n a warm Friday morning in September of 1983, my father climbed in his old red truck and drove away from the ranch in the foothills of Montana's Snowies. He was on his way to Roundup to haul home a load of coal, seventy miles there and seventy back. It was a trip he had made two or three times a year for thirty years. The weather had been dry and cloudless with all the endless false promises of fall in Montana, and he would have driven out of the shade of pines with the sun at his back, soon out of sight of the sandstone ranch house, the sawed-board corrals, and the warm sorrel back of his favorite mare, Kallie, grazing in the home pasture.

Seven miles down from the foothills, in Lewistown, he filled up at a self-service gas station on Main Street, and the manager—one of the last people who talked to him—said later that when he came in to pay her, he told her where he was going, and that he seemed happy to be on his way. Then he drove out of town, southeast.

The mine where he had bought his coal for so long is a few miles north of Roundup. Even in his slow old truck, he should have reached it in a couple of hours. But at dawn on

Saturday my sister Jackie called me in Havre to say that he never had stopped at the mine, never came home. Instead—from what we later were able to reconstruct—he drove past the side road and continued on Montana 87 into Roundup itself. Then he turned off the main street of Roundup onto Montana 12 to Forsyth and a part of the state he had never seen before. There is no logical accounting for his direction. The last time I was in Roundup, I circled back and drove through town a second time, showing myself how unlikely it would be for anyone to turn off the main street by accident or through confusion onto the Forsyth highway.

My sister and I knew nothing of this until much later. Although neither of us spoke it aloud, we both believed he had fallen asleep at the wheel and had rolled off the highway into some nameless, brush-choked coulee. My sister took my mother in with her and the children, while her husband spent the rest of the night driving and redriving the highway between Lewistown and Roundup.

But in fact, my father had driven to Forsyth and spent the night there in a motel. The next morning, Saturday, he paid his bill with a personal check and drove on east, away from home, angling south into some of the most sparsely settled territory in the world. And by midafternoon a report came to my sister—who had spent a sleepless night and a day making futile telephone calls to me, to the sheriff, to Search and Rescue, to me again—from the sheriff of Custer County, three hundred miles away, that he had been sighted at a remote ranch some thirty miles southeast of Miles City.

He had driven up to the ranch gate and stopped. I imagine him rolling down the window and scanning the miles of sagebrush and mirages between him and the horizon with the longsighted blue eyes of the cattleman, searching for signs of life, of movement.

The rancher, working around the place, noticed the strange

truck and felt uneasy about it—he had been robbed a few months earlier—so he went out to see what was up.

My father introduced himself by name. There followed a silence broken only, as I imagine it, by the wind rippling the sere September grass, a silence incomprehensible, perhaps, to anyone who has not lived in the western plains states. The two men would have waited, unhurried, the one in the cab of his dusty outfit, leaning his elbow out the window, the other with his arm on the gatepost, both of them dressed in their ordinary working clothes of scuffed boots and dirty Stetsons, Levi's, and ragged scarves, both of them with eyes not on each other but on the grass, the sky, the buildup of clouds and the approach of the first winter storm.

"If you'd met him," my cousin Willie told me later, "you'd have known he was another old Montana rancher like your dad, and the last thing he would have done was ask another man his business."

But the other rancher did begin to realize that, while he was in no risk of being robbed, he could not quite account for what he was seeing. "Anything wrong?" he asked, finally.

"No," said my father. He put his truck in gear and drove away, east and out of sight on a dirt road that would have led, eventually, to the South Dakota line. The other rancher, after mulling over the whole uneasy episode for several hours, decided to report it to the Custer County sheriff.

Jackie and I, going over and over this story, were relieved of our secret nightmares of the wrecked truck, the brushy gully, but we were perplexed by the direction and the purpose of our father's odyssey. What did he think he was doing? And why? *South Dakota?* A man who had preferred, all his life, to remain within twenty miles of his birthplace? What was he doing?

Still, we called our sister Betty in California to tell her that surely in a few hours we would have better news. Our father had been sighted alive and rational; surely he would be found soon, and we would know *why*.

But Saturday night fell, and with Sunday morning came the storm into eastern Montana. Rain and overcast and no further word.

"What was he wearing?" I asked Jackie over the phone.

"Long-handled underwear. And a wool shirt," she added.

We were silent, drawing what comfort we could from the thought of his wool shirt.

"Do you want me to drive down?" It was our unacknowledged code question.

"No. Not yet."

Every dragging hour meant less chance, and yet Search and Rescue, we learned, would not set out until a vehicle had been located. The heavy overcast in eastern Montana was keeping search planes on the ground. No word. No word.

What sustained us was not officialdom but the extended family network that had spread over the state. Cousins we had never met called their cousins in eastern Montana, and their children and relatives turned out, combing country roads and pastures on dirt bikes and on foot. Finally, on Monday afternoon, the persistent overcast began to lift, until cousin Willie, the pilot, could get his plane off the ground in Lewistown and head for Miles City. He spotted the red truck, and my father's body, within the hour.

"Do you want me to drive down?"

"Yes."

After the funeral, Willie drew my sisters and me aside to tell us what he had seen. Apparently my father had driven a few miles along the dirt road beyond the gate where he had talked to the other rancher, and he had parked the truck under a low hill overlooking a reservoir. In the distance he would have seen sage and sky, the blue outline of a butte, and the long blue bend of the Powder River. It looked a lot, Willie said, like the bend of the Judith River around the old homestead where my father was born and had spent his young manhood. It appeared as though he had gotten out of the truck and walked a few yards down the hill toward the reservoir, where a few cattle were grazing. Then he lay down on the slope and put his head on his arm as though to sleep.

My initial reaction to my father's death was less grief than a mixture of awe and rage. The awe was that he had achieved what Richard Hugo writes about in one of his last poems, "Death in the Aquarium."

> Where should we die given
> a choice? In a hothouse? Along a remote
> seldom traveled dirt road? Isn't some part
>
> of that unidentified man in us all
> and wants to die where we started?

My rage was at my father's acquiescence to that romantic and despairing mythology which has racked and scarred the lives of so many men and women in the West. The design by which he perceived his life can be traced clearly in his favorite books. During his last years he read and reread those old favorites—Louis L'Amour, Zane Grey, A. B. Guthrie—until it came to seem to me that his life was being transposed seamlessly into a chapter of the quiet rigor of *Arfive* or *The Last Valley*. I often wondered whether his fiction reading offered a pattern for his sense of himself, or a mirror. But so strongly did he believe in a mythic Montana of the past, of inarticulate strength and honor and courage irrevocably lost, that I cannot escape the conviction that a conscious choice shaped the way he died.

| | | | | | |

My father was born in 1913 in central Montana, near the mouth of Spring Creek where it flows into the Judith River, in his grandfather's two-story log house on the family homestead. His mother, my grandmother, had come out from Pennsylvania a few years earlier to teach at the Deerfield school and marry her cousin Albert.

Albert had become a legend by the time I could remember stories. He had been a cowboy, a top hand, had ridden rep for the old Huffine cattle outfit, under the old Open A L brand. As a child I heard how Duff Weir, the Scotchman who homesteaded the bench above our ranch, had counted at a branding while Albert hind-footed 167 calves before he missed one, and I knew with pride that, in the assessment of old-timers in central Montana, Albert had been the better breaker of a bronc to saddle, but my father was the better hand with a team of broncs.

In their formal wedding photograph, my grandmother in her handmade cream lace dress and her rimless glasses looks serene for once, her hands in her long kid gloves folded quietly in her lap. Albert sits behind her, leaning slightly toward her, solid in his fine dark suit and pale kid gloves. Both faces are mature, rather alike; they were first cousins. She looks directly out of the photograph, but Albert's eyes are fixed elsewhere, on some distant point, and he wears a slight, secret smile.

His seven younger brothers and sisters believed Albert could do anything. "Run him past me one time, Pete," he told the ten-year-old brother who had been riding and crying all afternoon, trying to corral a worthless ridge-running horse. So Pete ran the ridge-runner past Albert one time, and Albert's certain loop snaked out and front-footed him and snapped him head over tail, breaking his neck.

He was a fiddler; he played for all the country dances, including his own wedding dance. His fiddle hung in the attic of the stone house in the Snowies for years after mice gnawed away the soundboard. Probably a part of it still hangs there.

When my father was two years old, the gentle horse Albert was riding stepped in a prairie-dog hole and threw him, fracturing his skull. He recovered from the fracture, but a few months later, straining hard to lift a wagon out of a mudhole, he collapsed and was dead within a few days.

When I was five, my father bought back the home ranch on Spring Creek from his grandfather's estate. He was in his early thirties at the time, supporting his mother and his wife and two small daughters on an alkali spread on the lower Judith. I remember the suspense and the suppressed excitement as Grammy, daring to let herself hope, began to talk about the hay meadows and the old garden, the slough on the creek, and the peonies that had gone wild in the brush. For me at last came a day of upheaval and moving, and a night when I stood with my mother at the window of an unfamiliar kitchen. A kerosene lamp would have glowed beside us.

"Listen!"

It was the sound of cattle on the move. Soft, far away in the dark, unmistakable, unforgettable, a growing rumble, the bawling of cattle, and the yips of the riders. A primordial sound, swelling closer, a sound I would hear in my sleep, hear again and again as I grew old enough to ride and taste dust for myself and smell cattle. It was the sound of my father and his cousins, trailing the herd down through the river bluffs and home.

The home ranch lay between the Judith River and Spring Creek, stretching its pastures up the easy slopes of the South Moccasin Mountains. It had been buffalo country, with heavy grass and good water. Its landmarks were as familiar as a child's first awareness. To the north the flat blue outline of the butte overlooking the river, to the south the dusty point of the bench and the flash of silver that was the grain elevator at Danvers. On the slopes were the old corrals that Albert had built, but the ranch buildings lay under the bluffs in new territory for a child to explore. A two-track dirt road cut through the chokecherry grove that blossomed white in June and gradually bent under its heavy bunches of sour black fruit as summer wore on; led past the diamond willow with its low rough branches, where a child could climb; led over the low hill to the deserted old log ranch house with its back to the creek. Fresh water ran from the creek through the slough, and schools of minnows darted, almost invisible, under the boards of the footbridge. Mica sparkled from the cutbanks, and the red white-faced cattle grazed on the slopes in the sun, where the road twisted up through the bluffs, impassable in bad weather.

It was a grassland ranch, a cattle ranch. My father had built up his herd of old stock with the best registered Hereford bulls he could buy. He raised wild hay and stacked it with teams of horses, and he fed hay in winter with a team of horses and a sled. From late February he would be in the saddle from first light until long after dark, checking on his calving cows. The first sign of spring would be the night he rode in with the pale wet lavender of the first wild crocus, the pasqueflower, in his hatband.

A picture taken about this time shows the family on horseback in the big meadow below the ranch buildings. My father wears a light shirt, a dark vest, and chaps. His hat, characteristically, shades his face, obscuring it, but a cigarette juts white from the shadow, and the tilt of his shoulders, the angle of his stirrups, his seat on his big strawberry roan mare Sandy, are lines I would recognize instantly, anywhere, in my sleep. Beside him is my mother on Pardner, his top horse. My sister Betty and I, at ages five and eight, sit astride the gray ponies. Although it is a snapshot, it has the look of a posed photograph to enclose in letters to family in the East: *This is how we are.* My mother has turned toward Betty, who was afraid of her pony, but my father faces the camera, self-aware. He knows he is a cowboy.

Other snapshots of my father reveal his self-awareness.

Here is one where he poses his flashy team of sorrel colts at the water tank in a chiaroscuro of heavy shadows and dazzling light, like a poster of the West in black and white. Even in this other one, where he is caught off guard and half asleep by the flashbulb, while my little sister, the real subject of the picture taker, whirls around on the piano bench, he is self-aware; although his features, revealed here for once, are remarkably like Albert's.

"How very romantic those young men seemed to me," the wife of one of his cousins wrote recently to me. "I was a girl out of Spokane when I first met your father and Mel, and they were young cowboys, and they squatted on their bootheels and rolled their own cigarettes, and I had never seen anyone like them outside of movies."

Perhaps because he had no son, he raised his daughters as though we were boys. He dressed us in Levi's and started us on the ponies. If we got bucked off, we had to climb right back on. If, thrown off into dust or brush or rocks, we also lost the horse, it was our fault. We knew enough always to hang on to a bridle rein, no matter what. He put us to work in the corrals as soon as we were big enough, and by the time we were in our early teens he had us riding the broncs we had roped and hobbled and sacked out in the old cowboy way.

I remember starting out at dawn with him and his cousin Joe Murray to bring the cattle down out of the hills for branding, and how I shivered, envying the little hot flare of their matches when they cupped their hands and lit their cigarettes. And the way I imitated the line of his shoulders when he sat in the saddle, straightening my legs in the stirrups the way he did, remembering the story he had told me of old Jess Sample, who had seen him riding a mile away and said instantly, *That has to be Albert's son.*

He started working cattle with me when I was seven. I knew less about it than the dog did.

"Ride over across that coulee and haze down that old roan-faced cow with her calf," he might order as we rode, just as he would order Joe Murray.

Panic would set in. "What cow?"

"Can't you see her? The one with the Block H brand? She's about a quarter of a mile over there, back of that little clump of haws—"

I squinted, but it was no use. I needed glasses. Rather than admit to the blue blur that distance was for me, I would kick the pony into a trot in what I hoped was the right direction. The wrong direction would raise a bellow out of him, his arm waving me where I tried in vain to see.

I I I I I I I

But I didn't complain about riding with him all day, because when he was not yelling at me, he was talking. I listened as I rode with no more need to answer him than to interrupt the songs he sang tunelessly.

> *He built him a loop, a right nice loop,*
> *And he spread it good and true.*
> *He roped the devil round his pointed horns,*
> *And he took his dallies, too.*

"What are dallies?" I'd ask.

He would show me the two or three rapid wraps of the lariat around the saddle horn that he took between the time his loop settled over the calf's head and his line sang taut as the calf hit the end of it.

"There are boys that tie, but a tied rope's a good way to get your neck broke. You can always loosen a dally."

I tried roping the dog, but I usually missed.

My father told me the stories he had collected about Albert, and what it was like growing up in the footsteps of Albert's brothers, his brawling young uncles who inexplicably had deserted the ranch during the hard years of the thirties and gone to California to work for wages. He told about the winters before he was married, when he had batched with Jess Sample and run a trapline on the lower Judith.

He talked about the horses he'd owned. Juley, the gentle mare his mother had traded for when he was six. Banty, the pacing horse his uncle Pete had bought off the sulky circuit and given him to ride back and forth around the South Moccasins to the school at Duck Creek. Pet, the lovely sorrel that nearly died in the sleeping sickness epidemic of the 1920s, and Pardner, the wise brown gelding that had been so ungainly as a colt that he'd tried to trade him off to one of his cousins for a snakeskin hatband.

I listened, entranced, when he told about the cousin's fast mare, Baby, and how they had put together a relay string of Baby, Pet, and Pardner and won the relay race at the Fergus County Fair and Rodeo in 1937. I knew the rodeo grounds, and the mile dirt track in front of the rambling grandstand, and the announcer's platform over the bucking chutes; knew the crackle of the loudspeaker as a relay rider flogged his horse down the homestretch and tried to stop on a dime, his holder grabbing for his reins as he hurled himself off, snatched his saddle off his horse's back, and ran to throw it on his snorting, wild-eyed remount. My father said a really breakneck relay rider wouldn't bother to cinch his saddle; he'd vault onto his remount, throw his latigo over his shoulder, and thunder off.

My heart pounded to think of my father with a contestant's number pinned to the back of his shirt, riding in front of the grandstand while the roar went up, my father riding in the Grand Entry, with the Stars and Stripes rippling against the blue as the marshals rode the colors, the cowboys taking off their hats as the national anthem scratched on the loudspeaker. It seemed to me that the colors and the cheers had faded by the time I was born. My father was still glamorous, but now I was his only audience.

| | | | | | |

The price of beef cattle rose a little every year through the 1940s, and we lived on the fall cattle check and on our own beef and garden produce. Except for trips to Lewistown, like the halcyon one to celebrate the end of World War II, or to take in a day of the county fair, we saw few people outside the family. One of Albert's younger brothers, my uncle Theo, still ranched a quarter of a mile away, across the Judith River. A visit to him meant the breathless splashing trip across the current in the wagon behind one of the work teams. Occasionally Duff and Alec Weir drove down in their spring wagon. Otherwise it was my father and mother, Grammy and Bill Hafer, my little sister and me for months on end.

I learned to read at home and, my nose an inch from the page, read everything in sight. Even the strange old textbooks with nineteenth-century illustrations accumulated by my mother's mother from one-room schools all over Fergus County. Even the Hereford breeders' catalogs. Puzzling over the strange recurring names I found there: Domino. Mixer. Princess Mixer, Miss Mixer, Prince Domino. And the curious mail order advertisements for horn weights and emasculators. And the names of the breeders themselves: Bodley Herefords. Woodard and Sons.

"We'll be Jack Hogeland and Daughters," my father said.

But when my little sister turned five, my mother said, "I can't teach two of them at home. They've got to start school sometime."

We started at the Duck Creek school, where my father had gone. It was eight miles away, out of our district, but our own school lay on the other side of the Judith River and was out of the question. Getting us to Duck Creek meant a twice-daily drive, often through gumbo mud or snow. Our dirt road twisted up through the cutbanks, teetered along the edge of the bluffs, and cut across the prairie under the butte where the snow blew and drifted in the winter, when chaining up and shoveling through the drifts could make the trip an hour or more, each way. My father hauled gravel and improved the road, but it was precarious at its best.

And looming over us, closer every year, was the specter of high school in Lewistown.

Today the highways in Fergus County are oiled, and the schools are consolidated, and even very small children ride for hours in school buses in all kinds of weather. The choice my father made would be no choice at all today.

Many ranchers rented houses in Lewistown where their wives lived during the week while the children went to high school and the men stayed out on the ranches and fed the cattle. Others sent their high-school-age children to board alone in town during the winter, as my father himself had after finishing the eighth grade at Duck Creek. But my father could not bear the thought of such a separation from his own family.

He sold the ranch on Spring Creek and bought another, more marginal ranch in the foothills of the Snowies a few miles from Lewistown. Since it was so near the mountains, its summers were shorter and its winters harder, but it was on a Lewistown school bus route, and we could live at home and go to town schools.

He had three daughters now, the youngest named Jackie, after him, and he settled into the mountain ranch as best he could. The price of beef cattle plummeted, and he sold the Herefords and tried dairying. Tried sheep, tried a little logging. Nothing did well. The economy was changing, ranching was changing, and the cowboy grew more and more bewildered. Finally he gave up and leased out the pasture and went to work at the stockyards in town. Meanwhile my sisters and

I were riding down the gulch and back twice a day on the school bus and going to Fergus County High School and suffering a bewilderment of our own: the bewilderment of girls in the 1950s who have been raised like boys.

And then he lost us. One by one we finished high school and went away to the University of Montana. His plan for us was that we would become schoolteachers, like our mother and grandmothers, and that we would find country schools near home to teach during the winters (we'd have a little cash income, that way), and that we would live on the ranch during the summers and break horses and reclaim the hay meadows and even run a little stock again. But of course we did no such thing.

In my twenties, while I was in graduate school, I knew my father felt betrayed and angry. For years after I left Montana he would not even speak to me. But I had energy only for the rounds of seminars, research essays, teaching, and none at all for him. What I felt for him was anger that he had tried too hard to keep me tied to a tradition I saw as illusory. He had given everything he had for me; all I wanted was to be free of the cowboy.

The breach between us eventually, tentatively, eased into truce. His mind turned more and more to the past, to the lost grass slopes of the South Moccasins, and the gravel shallows of the Judith River, and its cutbanks and draws, as familiar and well-worn in his memory as the trunks and lower branches of diamond willows and box elders rubbed to satin by the backs of cattle. He went back over and over the sacrifice, remembering why he had made the choice, remembering the PCA (Production Credit Association) officer who had warned him not to do it, urged him to stay with what he knew.

The night before my father's funeral, in the hallway of Jackie's house, I noticed a knot of soiled clothes stacked on her washer.

"Father's clothes," Jackie said. "I brought them up here so Mother wouldn't have to see them."

The leg and thigh of his Levi's was streaked with mud, as though from a slip and fall. At the sight of that mud, the years rolled back, and I was in my early teens again, riding bareback for hours in the rain, looking for milk cows in a strange pasture, when I rode down a knoll through pines and found myself jolted over the head of my half-broken mare. Without warning, she had bogged her head and bucked.

I hit the grass rolling and wrapped my fingers in the wet reins so as not to lose her when she flattened her ears and jerked back. *Get right back on.* Talk her down, get a handful of mane, jump across her withers, scramble astride. She snorts, bogs her head again and bucks. She's slick with rain, bucking downhill. I don't stand a chance. I'm over her head again, rolling through something thorny. *Get right back on—* handful of mane, scramble over her withers, feel the earth coming up as she bogs her head again—*get right back on—* how long does it have to go on?

Seven, eight times. I had lost count when I looked up and saw my father watching me through the falling rain.

He had ridden out to look for me, in his hat and chaps and spurs, on Pardner, silent as a ghost through the gray curtain of rain. A white miasma rose from the creek behind him and swallowed his horse. For a moment I had to listen for the faint jingle of bridle chains to be sure he really was there. Then the mare lifted her head and whickered, and Pardner whickered back.

When cousin Willie told us, the next day, how he had found my father, I remembered how the mud had streaked my own legs; and I wondered then and wonder now, what did Willie really see, that afternoon on a dirt road southeast of Miles City? Or think he saw, or want us to believe he saw? None of us will ever know, not even Willie. The myth has its grip on us all.

LEAVING
MONTANA

Edna Hogeland, 1902, and Albert Hogeland, 1910.

| | | | | | | | | | | | | | | | | | | | | | | | | | | | | | | | | | | | | | | | | | | | | | | |

_O_n the fall of 1916 my grandfather, Albert Hogeland, saddled a horse and rode out across the slopes of the South Moccasins on an errand I have never heard named. He was thirty-three years old, a solid dark-haired man with the family blade nose and blue eyes, and he had grown up in the saddle. He had been a cowboy, a top hand, before he married and filed on his own homestead above his father's old place on Spring Creek; he had ridden rep for the old Huffine outfit in the twilight of the great cattle empires, and he was famous for his hand on a rope or a bronc. A Charles M. Russell watercolor of a cowboy throwing his weight into his stirrup against the plunge of the steer on the other end of his rope is said to be of Albert. Who knows? The cowboy in the watercolor is taut, concentrated on his moment. The brand on his horse is the old Huffine Open A L.

For the rest of their lives his widow and his surviving brothers and sisters spoke his name in a certain tone. _Albert_ was the name of calm, of a rock of strength. Albert, they said, could do anything. Blacksmith, carpenter, fiddler, poet. But after all the broncs he had ridden, it was a gentle horse he saddled that day in the fall, for whatever his purpose.

| | | | | | |

My cousin Joe Murray, on his way home to Montana from the West Coast in the summer of 1989, stopped for one night in Idaho with me. He and I sat in my living room above the Snake River and pored over old photographs and talked about the family until past midnight. Joe had brought along a photograph I had never seen before, of a posed group at a family picnic under the willows along Spring Creek, on the old Abe Hogeland ranch.

Judging from the women's dresses, the photograph had been taken in about 1910. Of the thirty or so picnickers lounging in the shade of the willows or sitting cross-legged in the grass or comfortably on chairs carried out from the house, Joe had identified about fifteen—"Though it's come to the point," Joe said, "when, if I say that's Grandpa, who's still alive to say it ain't?"

A few I recognized from other photographs. The still-faced woman in black, sitting in a chair under the trees, was certainly my great-grandmother Rachel.

"Look, Rachel," I said to my six-year-old, but she glanced at her namesake's face and ran out to play.

Women in white lawn and tight wrist-length sleeves and drooping bosoms. Obscure babies in unnecessarily heavy white shawls. Men with their faces stamped with the family likeness and burned dark from work in the hayfields. From the heavy grass under the willows, from the drooping leaves, the photograph would have been taken in midsummer. Possibly a Fourth of July picnic? Our family was fond of picnics on the Fourth, even in my time.

"My mother," Joe Murray pointed out. I studied the young face under the sailor brim, and yes, I thought I recognized her. She was Albert's youngest sister, Rebecca. My aunt Rebie.

"And Albert and Edna."

My grandparents sit in the grass in the foreground of the photograph, dead center. A tablecloth has been spread beside them. It holds the remains of the picnic, a plate of half-eaten layer cake as distinct as some of the shaded faces. Albert wears an open shirt and no hat; his eyes are light in his dark face, and his square hands are at ease on his thighs. She is in white, also hatless, laughing at him, just turning to the camera. Perhaps in the shape of her mouth, the tilt of her head, is something of the grandmother I remember.

In none of my photographs do Albert and Edna look so off their guard, so openly happy, and it occurs to me to wonder how long they have been married. Could they be just back in Montana from the ceremony in the East? Could the picnic be a celebration for them, the photograph a wedding commemoration? Certainly they are posed in its center; they are the focus.

Or is one of the white-swaddled obscure infants my father? As Joe pointed out, no one is left alive who could tell us.

I am drawn to Albert, his eyes, the strength of his hands. A blacksmith's hands, a fiddler's hands. They said he could turn his hands to anything.

He was born in Pennsylvania in 1882. His father, Abraham Hogeland, was a surveyor for the Northern Pacific Railway who went west ahead of the rails. In Montana Abraham resigned his position with the railroad, filed on the homestead at the mouth of Spring Creek, built a cabin, and sent for his wife and Albert. The seven younger children were born in Montana, but Albert was curious all his life about his native Pennsylvania. When his cousin Edna came out from Philadelphia to board with an uncle and teach at the Deerfield school, Albert courted her and traveled back east to marry her. Because marriage between first cousins was illegal in

Pennsylvania, they crossed the state line to New Jersey for the ceremony.

No daughter of mine will marry her first cousin, snorted their uncle Will at the time of Albert and Edna's marriage, but all four of his daughters did marry their first cousins. As a child I used to entertain myself plotting out the exact relationship between myself and my little cousin Punky, whose father had been my grandfather's brother, whose mother had been my grandfather's first cousin and also my grandmother's first cousin. Punky had four half brothers and sisters whose mother had been his mother's sister. When my father began taking my mother to the country dances, the family she boarded with warned her: *The Hogelands think they're too good to marry anybody but another Hogeland.*

| | | | | | | |

Typhoid had been rampant around Fergus County in the spring of 1917, and typhoid was listed as the cause of Albert's death. My father always speculated that the strain of struggling to lift that wagon out of the mud might have loosened a blood clot. On Albert's death certificate are written a few terse lines in ink: *cause of death unknown, no post mortem.*

Edna would have supposed her husband was recovering and safe from his skull fracture, only to lose him without warning. She was in her early thirties, her son barely three. She had the ranch with its good grazing but very little water, the sheds and corrals and barn that Albert had built, and the log house with the stone fireplace he had laid to draw well, but she had little else. And it was not her only bereavement. She had lost her only brother to tuberculosis, and at home in Philadelphia her father was newly dead. Her mother, Rachel, came out to Montana to help care for the little boy. Somehow the two women must have resolved not to return to Pennsylvania.

So in the spring of 1916, when the Model T chugged along the fresh ruts across the high slope toward the cluster of weathering ranch buildings, it would have carried with it a certain inevitability.

I I I I I I

The man was an Iowan who had made his way to Montana with the railroads, cooking for the construction crews. Small and spare, with the alert blue eyes and small beaky nose of a robin, he had left the rails at some time prior to 1916 and briefly hired on at the ranch to work for Albert. Probably he helped with seasonal work, haying or harvesting, for he, too, could turn a hand to many tasks, though unobtrusively and without style. He moved on when the work was finished; probably he would have moved on in any event, for he carried all the signs of the tumbleweed, the born bachelor so characteristic of his place and time in the West, working here and there and everywhere without roots or ties or ambition. Bill Hafer was his name. *That damned old Dutchman,* my grandmother came to call him.

He was cooking again in a railroad camp somewhere in Wyoming when word of mouth came that Albert Hogeland was dead, up in central Montana, and that Edna was alone. Bill asked for his time and headed north.

From Lewistown he would have taken the old stage road around the South Moccasins, down through the benches into the Judith River bottoms, past the Abe Hogeland ranch along Spring Creek, and back up the hill along treacherous ruts overhung with the wet white blossoms of chokecherries and hawthorns, climbing higher to the sagebrush slopes that looked across the river to the opposite benchlands, ten miles away, where the Weir brothers from Scotland had settled, to the railroad trestle diminished by distance and the faint rose shadow of the railroad station and post office at Danvers.

Higher on the slope ahead of him lay the familiar corrals and the shade of the diamond willow where the little boy played with a miniature barn, made of slats of wood from an apple crate sanded to satin and stained brown, an exact replica of the real barn a hundred yards away.

"Hello, Albert," said Bill, remembering his name, not knowing that everyone called this little boy Jack.

The nickname was a last legacy from his father. Disliking his own name, Albert had not wanted his son called after him. He liked the name Jack. Edna always claimed she had made a mistake. Following the baby's birth, when the doctor asked, "What's his name?" she thought he meant her husband and replied, "Albert Hogeland." That name was entered on the baby's birth certificate. Typically imperturbable, Albert called him Jack.

What Bill Hafer had come back to enlist in, whether he knew it or not, was a struggle for subsistence.

Edna's poverty during that time is not easily explained. It is true that the years following World War I were desperate ones for agriculture in Montana. Plummeting farm prices and the long drought of the 1920s would set off a population exodus from Montana whose numbers have never been completely reckoned. For the most part, however, the hardest hit were the newcomers, the honyockers who had flooded into Montana following the Enlarged Homestead Act of 1909 and tried to make a living on land that had been marginal in the first place. Settlers like the Hogelands, who had established themselves before the turn of the century along the choice creek bottoms, claiming the precious water, had a better chance. And prior to Albert's death there are no hints of the threadbare privation that Edna endured in the years following.

In choosing to stay in Montana, Edna had committed herself to the brunt of the work on the ranch. Rachel kept house and cared for little Jack; Edna worked outside. I, who grew up in the grinding tradition of the ranch work ethic, find it hard to imagine the will of that Philadelphia-bred woman that kept her rising, day after day, at three-thirty or four A.M. to feed her livestock and her chickens and milk her cows and then lug down the harnesses for her six head of workhorses and get them hitched to start her day in the field by first light. One foot after another, dust rising behind her harrow, wind sucking out the moisture, crops hardly realizing enough cash to pay for another season's seed wheat. Water for her livestock and her own needs and Rachel's and Jack's was pumped by hand from a well that might dry up any day. The springs already were drying up. The raspberries were dying. No fruit to eat, no fresh meat. Even the wild game had been hunted out of the country. Edna's teeth began to fall out.

By the time Jack was seven, he was putting in full days in the field, braced against the lines behind the workhorses until his young shoulders knotted with fatigue. His teeth, too, would fall out before he was thirty. "I liked to hear the sound of rain on the roof at night. Rain at night meant I didn't have to get up and go to work in the morning," he later told my sisters and me, and then he always added the caveat of the drylander: *Nobody who grows up in Montana should ever complain about the rain.*

When Bill Hafer came back from Wyoming, he pitched in beside Edna and her mother. One foot after another, falling back with every step they took, scratching not to get ahead or even to stay abreast but only to keep from sinking for as long as they could.

| | | | | | |

By the time I was ten, old enough to sense that a different woman once had breathed from the square weather-beaten frame of the grandmother I knew, Edna still retained a few possessions from the brief years of her marriage that seemed, even to a child, curiously alien to her life on the ranch.

Her sterling brush and comb and hand mirror, for example, weighted with elaborate Victorian silver roses and chrysanthemums, engraved with her initials. Her damask linen tablecloth, embossed with chrysanthemums, large enough for a seating of twelve, and her twelve matching damask napkins a yard square and hemmed by hand. Her surviving ladderback chairs with the rush seats, her cherry secretary were possessions that seemed like relics of a past so remote that their purpose had been forgotten.

For my mother, who scoured and painted and sewed curtains for every shack she ever lived in, who even bought cheap blue-flowered wallpaper and pasted it between the raw studs of the old granary we slept in one year, living with a woman who had long ago dismissed curtains was a constant irritant.

"She's never wanted anything," my mother fumed. "She doesn't want a house of her own. She'd just as soon live with us. She'd just as soon sleep with one of you girls—she doesn't even want her own bed. She didn't care about her house when she had one. When I married your dad and moved in with them, I found mouse dirt in her dish cupboard."

Edna was Grammy by this time. Grammy was short and broad, and she wore her thin gray hair scraped back from her face and wound in a small tight knot. Her feet, splayed and bunioned over the years, gave her a lot of trouble. She owned two pairs of shoes: the decent pair of black leather lace-ups with square heels that she wore to town or to visit her relatives, and the older pair, splitting over the corns, that she wore to do chores or field work, whatever my father needed done on the ranch. Grammy hated to do housework; she would fling a meal on the table any which way, but she would grind away all day in the hot sun with a pair of posthole diggers and a shovel, setting new posts along the river where the fence washed out every spring, or she would shovel wheat or help butcher. She lived to work for my father, and she kept her pace well into her seventies. Her strength seemed limitless.

When I was thirteen, I came home from high school bragging about learning to arm-wrestle in PE. I was a strong, hardworking ranch kid, and I had arm-wrestled all my daintier poodle-cut and pearled classmates and won.

"Let me show you, Grammy."

She laid down her fork and leaned across the supper table to clasp my hand. It was like arm-wrestling with one of her own cedar posts. Without a quiver, without seeming to flex her stringy arm, she pinned mine to the table.

A bleached color snapshot from the 1950s shows Grammy in the branding corral in her square shoes and her starched percale dress, about to throw her rope over a calf's head. She sunburned easily, and perspired, and she bled easily from every tiny scratch. In the summers her face blistered and peeled, and her arms were crosshatched with the tiny black-beaded wounds of barbs and thorns.

Grammy, when she could be caught between chores, was an indefatigable reader-aloud. Laying aside the knitting she snatched up every time she sat down, leaning back in her rocking chair with a granddaughter in her lap, she would drone her way for the fourth or fifth or eleventh time through the scanty supply of storybooks we possessed. The REA (Rural Electrification Administration) had strung its miracle wires as far as the ranch by that time, and she read to my little sisters and me by electric light, not kerosene. Books were the evidence we had of a world outside the ranges of mountains that enclosed central Montana, and we knew ours nearly by heart: our cherished collection of birthday and Christmas books, the discarded readers and outdated geographies brought home by our other grandmother from the country schools she taught in, the tattered survivors of our father's childhood or Grammy's young womanhood. *Laddie* and *The Harvester. St. Elmo. Mary Cary. The Lady of the Lake. The Five Little Peppers and How They Grew.* The *Just So Stories.* A curious mirror of the world, a curious contrast with what we knew. A few years later my mother got us library cards at the Carnegie City Library in Lewistown, and we hauled home armloads of books and imagined that somewhere lived people who acted and talked like the ones we read about.

If we ran out of books, Grammy told us stories. She described the rural lane of her childhood, near Philadelphia, and the millpond where she and her brother, Elias, had tormented the miller by throwing stones into the millrace until he rushed out, screaming, *B'ys! B'ys! No stones!* She told us about the unruly cow her father had kept, and how she and Elias chased it from lane to pasture until at last she caught it by the tail—*Hangin' on a cow's tail!* Elias jeered until their father shut him up. *Edna brought the cow home, didn't she?*

And the Sunday afternoons when an uncle used to bring salt and fresh lemons and a barrel of oysters to the house in Philadelphia, and what a treat the raw oysters right from the barrel were for her and her sisters and Elias—

"Ick!" we always said. We were little prairie-bred girls.

"In Montana we eat beef," my father said, incensed by such effete eastern habits as eating oysters.

—and how Elias came west in hopes that the thin air would cure his tuberculosis, and how he herded sheep for his uncle Abraham in the rain. Elias's was the first grave, Grammy said, in the Lewistown cemetery.

Grammy could tell stories as she worked. I followed as she laid out feed for the milk cows or drove new staples in a fence, listening as she told how Great-grandfather Abraham had chosen this exact spot for his homestead, and how his wife, Mary, had traveled west by stagecoach to join him with her two-year-old son, Albert, in her arms, and about the night the driver got so drunk he upset the stage with all its passengers. Hearing no sound from the little bundle in her arms, fearing the worst, my great-grandmother screamed and woke the soundly sleeping baby. Grammy pointed out the old stage road to me, where the accident happened, and I can see it yet, a line of dense weed growth along the base of the South Moccasins, when I drive from Fort Benton to Lewistown.

The next year the second of their eight children, Carrie, was born in their cabin. She was the first white girl baby born on the Judith River, the family always said. Cowboys rode for miles, or so the story went, for the chance to see little Carrie, so starved were they for the sight of a baby.

"Carrie is the one most like her mother," everybody said.

As Grammy plodded back and forth behind the stacker team, raising load after load of hay to the top of the stack in the shade of the twelve giant cottonwoods, she explained how my great-grandmother had so loved the grove that the boys had left them standing in the middle of what was now our biggest hay meadow when they cleared away the rest of the brush and trees, to be called ever after the Grandma's Trees. And she told about the hard winter of 1887 and how in the spring of that year Great-great-uncle Theo, Abraham's brother, had walked for the first time along Spring Creek toward the river and his future ranch and said he could have walked all the way on the carcasses of frozen cattle.

And the time Albert was drawing his plans for the log house on the slope, and she said, *I want a window here, and here, and another window here—* Nobody had that many windows in those days, but she wanted windows everywhere. . . .

Today the story about the house with windows strikes me as an odd one to be told by the woman who cared nothing for houses. What had become of her younger self? Grammy's stories lit up moments, fragments, but they contained no conclusions. Overhearing them, Bill Hafer's dry little chuckle sometimes escaped him, but he never added to her accounts or told any of his own. Cards were Bill's forte. He had played cards around the railroad camps in his youth, and in the winter my sisters and I sat around the table with him and Grammy while he counted us out little piles of navy beans to bet with and dealt us hands of stud poker.

Eventually my sister and I would lose our beans and fold our cards, but Grammy hung on, peeking grimly at her hole card and glaring at Bill. He would have something showing, a pair of queens maybe, nothing to beat her aces. But what did he have in the hole?

Bill would wait, smiling his meaningless little smile, ready to deal her another card.

She studied her own hand, studied his, studied his face. Was he bluffing? Only one way to find out. She raised him her last three beans.

Bill turned over his hole card as we crowded up to see. Sure enough, he had the third queen. As Grammy leaned over to look in disbelief and outrage his dry chuckle escaped him again.

She flung her cards at him. "You goddamned old Dutchman! You do it every time! Every single time! If I don't raise you, you're bluffing, and if I do, you're not! See if I ever play cards with you again!"

And she would stalk off, muttering to herself, fuming, while he laughed and laughed and reshuffled the cards.

| | | | | | | |

Bill is a constant in my life from my earliest recollections. At the time I was born, my parents and Grammy and Bill were living on a ranch on the lower Judith; they had starved out on the high slope. We lived in the house made of cottonwood logs set on a sagebrush flat. A box elder tree grew in the yard, and the river curved and sparkled under the cutbank.

Grammy-and-Bill. Old Hafer-Bill. He carries the slop bucket in one hand, leads me by his other hand on the walk down to the pigpen in the evening. Going with him to feed the pigs is one of my favorite excursions. But on the way home through the milk cow pasture, my legs get tired.

"Bill! Carry me!"

"I have to carry the bucket."

"I'll carry the bucket, and you carry me."

He laughs, delighted.

He will quarter apples for me, put his glasses on and read to me by kerosene light, or draw pictures of pigs for me.

"P-I-G spells hog," he says.

It hardly occurs to me that all little girls don't have a Grammy-and-Bill living with them.

| | | | | | | |

Between Bill and my mother existed an unspoken alliance. Neither of them was a Hogeland. And my mother felt sorry for Bill, resented the lack of consideration and care he got from Grammy. When, laid up with blood poisoning in his leg, he complained that he couldn't eat the food in St. Joseph's Hospital, it was my mother who cooked his favorite meals and smuggled them past the sisters.

For his part, Bill occasionally dropped a word in my mother's ear.

"Hope Jack don't let anybody buy that ranch of his granddad's too cheap," he remarked one afternoon.

My mother glanced at him. She was driving the truck to Danvers for the mail, with my little sister and me squeezed between her and Bill in the cab. Bill sat with his elbow out the window, watching the sweet clover whip by. His small red poker face was bland behind his glasses.

"Yes," said my mother slowly.

I was all ears. With the acute antennae of childhood, I

knew something was up. But neither of them said another word. It was years before my mother told me more of the story.

My great-grandfather had died intestate. More than one of the heirs wanted the ranch on Spring Creek, which was being sold, and feeling in the family was running high. Bill was loyal to my father and grandmother, but he didn't mind seeing the rest of them done in the eye. He had resented their treatment of Edna after Albert's death, my mother said. He believed that one of Albert's brothers had taken advantage of her, appropriated machinery and stock that had been Albert's, and shortchanged her in hay and grain.

For Grammy, the family could do no wrong. But—"After what Bill said, I got to thinking," my mother told me. She, too, harbored resentments. *The Hogelands think they're too good for ordinary folks.* "I told your dad, why should we care what the family says? We've got as much right to submit a bid as the next one."

So my mother threw her weight into the tug-of-war over my father that lasted until Edna's death, and, backed by the cash of his old Scottish neighbors, the Weir brothers, my father submitted a bid. His was the top bid, and his grandfather's ranch was his. It added hay meadows and water from Spring Creek for irrigation to the high pastureland that had been Albert's. It was a new beginning, a chance for better things, and I remember their elation.

Most of Abraham's surviving children, my great-aunts and uncles, still lived within a twenty-mile radius of the old homestead. Carrie, the sweet-tempered, had raised eight children of her own on a ranch near Sample's Crossing. Her sons had broken colts and swapped colts and ridden in relay races with my father. Rebie, the hotheaded sister, raised four unruly boys in town. They spent their high school summers with my father on the ranch. Bess, the serious sister, and Pete and

Barney, the brawlers, had gone to California, but Frank was the Lewistown city engineer and Small Theo (to distinguish him from Great-great-uncle Theo) ranched just across the Judith River from us. They all seemed elderly to me, but as stable and familiar as the stars as they went about their lives, visiting each other, quarreling, and keeping track of kinship down to the third and fourth cousins.

My mother always baked cakes and rolls for the family celebrations, and Grammy hugged and kissed her sisters-in-law whenever she met them, and they tried to kiss me, and I rode horseback with second and third cousins and played in irrigation ditches and climbed in the willows and raided magpie nests. It was a mild surprise in those days to meet someone I was not related to.

Still, a fissure was widening. When I remember those big Christmas celebrations and branding bees and Fourth of July picnics, it is as an outsider. Gradually our little family was becoming isolated.

Why? I now wonder. Was it wholly over property and inheritance? Did my mother's touchiness stir the old resentments?

Which of the family had Edna offended after Albert's death, when she resolved to stay in Montana and grind away her days plowing and harrowing and seeding behind six-horse teams? Were her sisters-in-law as put out as my mother by her disregard for housekeeping, her sloppy ways, her love of outdoor work, her easy assumption of men's labors? Were the unforgiving family mores outraged because, in her own fashion, she had married Bill Hafer? Or because she never married him?

Surely in returning to Montana, lending himself to the backbreaking dawn-to-dark work of staying alive on the ranch, Bill Hafer would have expected to marry Edna. It was a commonplace plot of western settlement. But he did not marry her. He never married her or anybody else, although he stayed with her for forty years.

⟨ | | | | | | | ⟩

My mother's voice: *I always thought she felt she was too good to marry him. She was a Hogeland. She'd keep him around and let him work for her, but she wouldn't marry him.*

No, the family didn't like it, the way she lived alone with him out there on the ranch after her mother died. There was talk. They worried about Jack.

She never slept with him as far as I knew. They each had their own bedroom, sometimes just a blanket hung between them for a curtain. Once, when he was laid up with his leg, I took a tray up to him, and she was lying on the bed beside him with her clothes on, holding his hand.

| | | | | | |

Grammy-and-Bill. Sometimes, when there was work to be done, like a branding, he went along to the family doings. Other times he went off on private, never disclosed errands of his own. He is not present in the photograph of the family lined up on the minister's front porch after my parents' wedding, although he sat through all the interminable country school Christmas programs and piano recitals my sisters and I ever performed in. He had a little money of his own by then. Grammy and my father had signed the ranch on the lower Judith to him at the time of the move to the home ranch, and he sold it and lived on the payments. My sister and I were named in his will as his heirs.

I recall his face as clearly as Grammy's, his shiny glasses and his beak of a nose and the tilt of his little straw hat as he came home from one of his errands, lugging a treat for us all, perhaps a watermelon or a flat of strawberries. After forty years, why would he not be a permanent fixture?

In the early 1950s Bill was hospitalized in Great Falls. He must have been at least seventy, and he had had trouble with his leg for years. This time the specialist told my parents he had cancer. Although I was old enough by then to be aware of such things, I was never told the nature of the cancer or the treatment. Probably cancer of the prostate, which would explain the silence about it; probably an orchiectomy. What I do remember is that we made the rare trip to Great Falls and drove through the luxurious shade of its tree-lined streets, and that, on the hundred-mile drive home, my father was so shaken by the diagnosis that he pulled off the highway and asked my mother to drive. Bill, he said, was the closest to a father he had ever known.

But the bonds were to be stretched, stretched until finally they snapped. After the diagnosis, Bill became restless. He bought himself a Studebaker with some of his money and disappeared for weeks at a time.

"You won't have a dime left of your money at the rate you're going!" Grammy raged at him when he showed up again. She could not understand his quest, could not stop him, could not quite believe she could not. Bill listened while she lectured him, his head cocked, his glasses shining out of his little poker face. In the morning he would be gone again.

Grammy was right about his money. Besides the Studebaker, he bought a Geiger counter. It was about the size and weight of a truck battery; it hung from his neck by a strap, and it had a dial and a needle that wavered. He thought he might find some uranium down along the Missouri River. Instead, he found a woman on a remote ranch in the Missouri River breaks, and he moved in with her for a while. She thought she might be able to make money raising irrigated strawberries if she just had some start-up cash. The woman had a daughter in her teens. On one of Bill's trips home, he pulled an order form from a Sears catalog from his pocket. The girl had filled it out. I read it and wondered about her, living out in the breaks, miles from nowhere, waiting and hoping for pretty clothes.

Bill may already have forgotten about her. He was feeling worse, and he turned to the faith healers. To Grammy's outrage, their letters and brochures began to arrive in each week's mail. The healing power of prayer, mud baths, hot springs, more prayer. He got letters from Oral Roberts. If he could just send more money . . .

But he was running short of money. He began selling his possessions, his odds and ends of machinery, at a local auction barn. The Geiger counter went. Then he hunted around the ranch for anything he could sell for a dollar or two as scrap iron, and one of the things he found to sell was a blacksmith's anvil that had been Albert's. The anvil was gone before my father missed it; when he did, he burned with the disbelieving fury of one who has been run over by someone else's obsession. He could never forgive it.

That was that. Bill packed what he had left to pack in his old Studebaker and drove away. My mother stripped his bed and threw out the rusted juice can he had been using as a pissoir and began storing the household overflow in the cubbyhole that had been his room. Grammy grumbled about him for a few more months, but he was gone.

How quickly the space dissolves that so recently was vacated. I don't remember grieving for Bill. Probably I was glad to see the last of him—although, of course, none of us knew it was the *last time*. He'd come and gone on his own secret errands for years; he might come and go again. Old Hafer-Bill. I was in high school by then, and the differences between me and the town girls felt like stigmata. I didn't know how to answer the question *Who's Bill?*

Gradually the smells of the part of the house that had been Grammy-and-Bill's, of their chamber pots and shoes and their cups for soaking their false teeth and their seldom bathed old bodies, became hers alone. After a few years, my mother got a letter from Iowa, from Bill's last living blood relative, a niece. Bill had died, the niece wrote. He had never given up looking for a miracle cure for his cancer. When he died, he had three hundred dollars, and she had used it to buy him a tombstone.

Grammy seemed hardly to notice his death. Perhaps she didn't notice, for she was beginning to turn inward. She, too, was disposing of her possessions. As though reliving the years of scratching to put off for as long as possible the inevitable day of starvation, she tried to sell her last pieces of silverware. She sent boxes to the auction barn until my mother noticed what she was doing and took to sorting through them to retrieve the cut-glass salt cups, the bone-handled knives.

One day she would be fondling a bundle of Albert's letters and poems, the next day they would be missing. She seemed not to know my father. She believed that strangers were visiting her, sitting in her chairs around her table.

My father could not bear to watch her decline. In her distress, Grammy turned to her old adversary, my mother, the one person whom she was sure to recognize from the depths of her final self-absorption. It was my mother who chased away Grammy's invisible visitors with her broom, who reported on her conversations with the long dead, and told how, seeing a child, she became convinced that she had lost a little boy.

Grammy had given me the damask tablecloth when I was married, and some of the coin silver spoons with her monogram, those few artifacts from that long-ago young womanhood in Philadelphia which somehow had survived the drought years and the dreadful years. In turn I carried them around for decades, through married student housing and trailer parks in the Midwest and high-rise rentals on the West Coast, through upheaval and divorce and, years later, remarriage: the enormous, lustrous tablecloth and the silver spoons so soft that one of the smallest, engraved with Rachel's initials, had been indented by a teething baby.

An anvil, a few guns, silver spoons and a tablecloth. The artifacts that, like my grandmother's stories, illuminate moments but lack conclusions. The tokens that tell us when we're still in the game, that tell us when we've been dealt out by those on the one-way road ahead of us. After all these years, I see my father's face, imprinted with the loss of his anvil with lines as deep as the scored dirt floor of the log shed where it had been sitting the day before. After all these years, I feel his rage as he stares at the deep-embedded rectangle of its absence, then turns in the dim light in growing surmise toward the blaze of sun at the low door of the shed, realizing his new loss and the old as he strides into the sunspots until his dark retreating outline is lost in the glare.

LITTLE JAKE
AND THE OLD WAYS

Jack Hogeland with Pet, 1937.

‖‖‖

*A*s the violence of the Reformation lit fires in central Europe during the sixteenth century, an Austrian Anabaptist named Jacob Hutter died for refusing to recant his formal confession of faith. Unlike so many men and women, Catholics and Protestants, who died in the flames of religious conviction, Hutter had not sought martyrdom. Years earlier he had led small bands of Anabaptists from persecution in Austria to the relative safety of Moravia, where they settled in their characteristically austere, isolated communes until 1535, when a shift in political power shattered their flimsy security. Hutter and his wife were taken prisoners. Though tortured, he was steadfast; finally, on February 25, 1536, he was burned at the stake.

Hutter's followers—condemned by Luther for their monastical withdrawal from the world, hunted out of their isolated communes in Moravia during the Thirty Years' War, burned alive, drowned in grim irony at their insistence on adult baptism—retreated through Slovakia and paused for a century in the Ukraine, a remnant population of eight hundred souls, before retreating again in 1874 from the threat of military conscription. This time the Hutterites looked for solace on the American homestead frontier. Asking only to be let alone, to live and bring up their children in their old ways, they came, all eight hundred of them, first to South Dakota and then to Montana, where they had a few years before the outbreak of World War I to begin to reconstruct their communes according to their ancient pattern.

| | | | | | |

Jacob Hutter had left his followers an unremarkable, quiet legacy: a handful of epistles and a tradition of pacificism that has survived against all odds into the twentieth century. It is a tradition that forms a curious chain from Hutter's agony at the stake in 1536 to the incarceration of a young man, in the 1970s, in a root cellar in central Montana.

Here, unexpectedly, from an old issue of *National Geographic,* surfaces the face of that young man. "Note 'Little Jake' on the right side of the picture," my sister wrote in the margin of the copy she lent me, but I would have known Jake anywhere: snub-nosed, familiar, leaning into the rising curl of smoke from the branding iron, his cowboy hat at a cocky angle as he concentrates on what was an ordinary day's work to him but must have looked exotic to the *Geographic*'s photographer.

The text describes Jake's colony as a colorful anachronism on the western plains and explains how, through their own decency, these "plain people of the west" have overcome the prejudice of their neighbors. And yet, turning pages, I feel a stab of anger. These are my mountains, my South Moccasins. This is home, my home ground. I grew up on this ground, rode across this very slope. *Mine.* And yet these people know the ground. They have made themselves at home, even though the place used to be mine.

Jake's face appears in the photograph of cattle branding

by accident. He is never mentioned; he would be a discord in this text. But like Hutter, his first name was Jacob. "Little" Jake they called him to distinguish him from the other Jakes of the colony (we also knew Big Eli, Young Joe, Old Paul), but Jake was little in fact, five-six and wiry, like a cowboy. His surname could be traced back to the handful of believers who saw Jacob Hutter burn.

History is a bad joke. Consider, for example, how the Hutterites arrived on the Montana homestead frontier just in time to become targets for Montana's anti-German hysteria on the threshold of World War I. Or how, after still another exile of thirty years in Canada during and between the two world wars (a mere gulp of breath in their long history of displacement), the Hutterites recrossed the border into Montana in 1946 only to blunder up against cowboys.

On the one side were the Hutterites, busy and self-absorbed as ants in their sober black clothing, chattering among themselves, frantically furrowing and building to make up for their hundreds of lost years. On the other side were the lonely, obsolete cowboys, living out the last of their tradition according to their unwritten rules of horsemanship and conduct, their notions of honor, and their immolation of themselves to an ideal transmitted through popular literature and film. Theirs was a clash less of cultures than of faiths, a standoff between primitive Christian communism and offended silence and twilight invulnerability. The noisy Hutterites unwittingly violated the code of the West every time they drew a breath of prairie air.

The Hutterites in many respects were no different from other ethnic groups who settled the homestead frontier and only a little more conspicuous. Italians who had come to Montana to work on the railroads sent for their families and tried to keep their children and their language and their church to themselves. Whole communities of Swedes and Norwegians had left their stony, narrow pastures along the fjords and come to look for fertile farm ground, and they brought along their own pastors and yammered among themselves in their incomprehensible singsong. Croatian stonemasons came to central Montana and built half the establishments on Lewistown's main street from blocks of dressed sandstone. Other central Europeans—Catholic Czechs, Moravians, Slovaks, Bohemians, known collectively and indiscriminately to their Protestant neighbors as *Bohunks*—flocked into Montana during the great homestead migration of 1910 to 1914, often by the whole, intact village, and withstood the fearful vacancy of the prairie as best they could by settling next to each other.

Race aroused a deeper dread on the frontier than the mere suspicion of an alien language or religion, and a worse menace than Bohunks to white settlers was the Asians who had come to the Montana Territory during the gold rush, first to work the tailings of the mines, later to lay railroad ties or operate laundries or small groceries. The presence of the Chinese in Montana generated a miscegenation law that was not repealed until the 1960s. Most Asians, however, had disappeared from the state by 1910, and it became possible to pretend they had never existed. In 1988 one local history committee, compiling a commemorative volume in honor of Montana's centennial celebration of statehood, listed their county's 1888 census of donkeys but decided to omit any reference to its substantial 1888 population of Japanese railroad workers.

The Indians had been herded out of sight on reservations by the beginning of the twentieth century, but another remnant population—the Métis, the *Breeds*—lingered in the cottonwood log cabins to remind even the most venerable white settlers of the older culture they themselves had displaced. The Métis, those buffalo-chasing descendants of French fur traders and Cree women, had carved deep ruts down across the prairie from the north with their wooden-wheeled carts and established a permanent colony on Spring Creek, in present-day Fergus County, years before territorial entrepreneurs moved in, renamed the settlement Lewistown, and hired Croatians to replace the cabins with sandstone banks and stores and mansions on streets whose names—Janeaux, Ouellette—oddly recalled an otherwise repudiated past.

| | | | | | | |

For me, that first glimpse of radical otherness came in the fall of 1946 when, playing in the yellowing willows along the fence, I glanced up and saw strange riders at the corral gate.

I saw hardly anyone outside my family from one month to the next, and even a chance visit from a neighbor in search of strayed cattle was likely to send me into hiding. Riders at the corral gate, therefore, would have halted my play under any circumstances—but so many, and so outlandish in their black clothing and shapeless black hats! Did they stop? Were they passing through? I couldn't have said. I saw them through a dark haze; I had gone to cover in the willow leaves like a coyote pup.

"The Mennonites are back," my Pennsylvania-bred grandmother said.

"Hutterites!" everybody corrected her, but she kept right on calling them Mennonites. I thought she said *midnights*. The word fit the darkness, the threat of the riders I had seen. The *midnights* rode through my sleep in the tangled manes of nightmare, and I woke to adult voices speaking of outrage.

"It used to be," my father said bitterly, "in this country, that you could leave your house unlocked, saddles in the barn, tools around the place, and you didn't have to worry. Wasn't a man in the country that would touch a neighbor's property. Then those sons of bitches came along, just before the first world war. They'd ride through a place, and if nobody was around, they'd take shovels, buckets, ropes, Christ almighty, anything that wasn't nailed down."

"Are these the same guys that used to live up at the old colony?" asked my cousin Joe Murray. He had been living at the ranch and working for my father ever since he got mustered out of the navy.

"No, hell, that was thirty years ago. This is a younger bunch, for the most part. The preacher, though, I think he might be one of the original outfit. He's a lot of their trouble. They have to do whatever he says. They can't do a goddamned thing on their own."

"All the Hutterite men have to grow beards after they get married," my mother had explained when I asked her about it.

"Why?"

But she hadn't known that. "Just part of their religion, I guess."

The colony lay along Spring Creek, a few miles upstream from our ranch. I had never seen it, but I had imagined it as an unnatural humming swarm on the slopes of the South Moccasin Mountains, a dark place that spewed dark riders. Now a dire, bearded old man glared holes in the backs of my eyelids.

| | | | | | | |

The furbearing Christians, some called the Hutterites, equally incensed at their hairy faces and their conspicuous religious practice in a plains culture that valued privacy to the point of paranoia. But worse than the Hutterites' broad-daylight observance of their own religious precepts was their incomprehension of ours.

Between trying to keep Hutterite cattle out of our winter pasture, which bordered theirs, and worrying about which of our yearlings might find its way into that walk-in freezer plant at the colony, my father stayed furious all that winter and into the next summer and fall. The thirty-year-old line fences between us and the colony were falling down. *Yes, and they're the only sonsabitches in the country that don't or won't understand what it is to be neighbors—by God, if they can't keep their fences up and their cattle out and their kids from riding through other men's places, they don't deserve good neighbors. For all their goddamn pious carrying on, they don't have no idea in the world what it means to be a white man.*

Hutterite cattle broke through the rusting wires and invaded us time after time. Almost every week Joe and my father would have to haze off a little bunch of Hutterite cattle grazing our slopes. Or else the old Scotch bachelor brothers from up on the bench would stop in their spring wagon to tell us there were Hutterite cattle in the wheat. Then Joe and my father would have to saddle up again, no matter what pressing work they had to leave undone, for the Hutterites would not (or could not, as my father finally perceived after several furious, futile rides up to the colony to yell at them) drive their own cattle home.

One night he and Joe were laughing when they rode home. My father told how they had spent the afternoon sitting their horses on a knoll and watching as a dozen Hutterites, understanding the necessity for cowboying but failing to get the hang of it, tried to catch one of their yearling strays.

"Those Hoot kids would ride like hell until they caught up with the calf," my father said, "and then they'd leap off their horses and try to catch him on foot. Naturally the calf would outrun them, so they'd climb back on their horses and chase him down again. Then off they'd leap to run him some more on foot. We sat there and laughed at those dumb sonsabitches until we damn near died."

But their friendliness! To his further disbelief and outrage, the Hutterites actually seemed to like him. None of his retorts was curt enough, no shoulder he turned too cold to daunt the gold-toothed smiles that broke all over their furry faces whenever they ran into him in town or cornered him at a sale. "Jack! Jack!" they greeted him. "Jack, vot is the grass like? Vot are ve going to do for rain?"

Smothered with the radiant regard of the older men, with the admiration of the pinched-faced boys who watched to see how he swung into his saddle or wore his spurs, my father seethed, but he was helpless; it was as though cats were rubbing against his legs and he couldn't quite bring himself to kick them.

But then one night at supper my father remarked to my mother, "They got a kid up at the colony now that's a pretty good hand."

A good hand. In the twilight of the cowboy culture, what could be higher praise?

For a Hutterite kid in the late 1940s, beginning to get his bearings on the slopes of the South Moccasins, what praise could be more seductive?

| | | | | | |

"Jack, you ain't seen a yearling calf run through here draggin' a almost new lariat rope?" the Hutterite kid had asked him.

So began a conversation I never heard, never heard retold until years after the idea of Jake had taken a shape of its own in my father's version of the episode. Did it take place? But it must have, if not word for word as my father remembered it, at least in outline—whether my father, turning around from his tinkering on some rattletrap piece of machinery or pausing to close a wire gate, saw the shadow of the horse fall across the bunchgrass before he looked up and saw the black-clad fifteen-year-old boy mounted on the horse's back or, reining in his own brown gelding Pardner, met the boy's eyes: the whiplash man in his late thirties, famous locally for his hand on a bronc, and the raw-faced, undersized boy who had known his name.

"Jack, you ain't seen a yearling calf draggin' a almost new lariat rope?"

"No," said my father, biting off the word in disdain. He would have looked beyond the boy as though, by averting his eyes, he could dissolve him out of the landscape.

Jake persisted. "If you see a yearling like that, will you safe my rope for me, Jack?"

Then my father did look at him, in pure blue disgust. "Hell, yes!" he said. "I'll save your almost new rope for you, just like you furbearin' sons of bitches would save my almost new rope for me, if I was damn fool enough to rope a calf with it and then let him get away."

"Oh, de hell," said Jake right back at him. "I'd safe your almost new rope for you, Jack."

"The hell you would," said my father, but he had been taken aback enough by Jake's cocky cowboy style to realize he was talking to a boy, after all, even if this snub-nosed boy did have to choke up the English from the back of his throat.

Jake grinned, sure of himself now. "You'll safe it for me if you find it, Jack!"

"Hell no, I'll keep it!"

"My rope?"

"No, the yearling calf!"

After the first startled second, Jake laughed out loud, and my father laughed with him.

| | | | | | |

It is curious that westerners, so tolerant of the eccentric, the loner, or the crazed, so ready to make a folk hero out of a Butch Cassidy or a Long George Francis, can simultaneously harbor such dread of cultural difference—although perhaps it is inevitable that westerners, made up entirely of displacers, should fear displacement. And economic displacement by the industrious, collective operations of the Hutterites, who would do without all manner of personal necessities or small pleasures in order to buy miles of prime land and top-of-the-line equipment to farm it with, eventually became a reality for some marginal ranchers.

Unlike the Czechs and Croatians and Moravians who had sent their children to public schools and seen them learn how to blend in with other children and make fun of the language of their parents and the customs of the old country, the Hutterites were determined to keep their children true to their own. To keep their children, to support their new families, to operate their own colony schools for the legal minimum of eight grades, to maintain the self-sufficiency that allowed them to live apart and unto themselves, they badly needed more land for new colonies.

Angry ranchers would make—and break—pacts not to well out to the Hutterites. Here, for example, is an item from the Lewistown *Daily News* of March 27, 1952:

HUTTERITES BUY HOGELAND RANCH NEAR DEERFIELD

The Jack Hogeland ranch near Deerfield has exchanged hands twice since early last November, it has been learned here.

Hogeland first sold his property, which lies on both sides of the Judith River and adjoins the Spring Creek Colony, to Alvin E. Peterson of Martinsdale. The purchase was made on a contract for deed transaction.

Then early this year, Peterson sold the ranch to the Spring Creek Colony, according to Jacob Walters, head of the colony. The sale was also on contract for deed.

Jack Hogeland said this week he refused to sell his ranch to the colony when approached on the matter. Later, however, he sold to Peterson.

I was afraid of the stout old men with their long whiskers when I saw them on the sidewalks of Lewistown on a Saturday afternoon (which was the preacher?), but I watched the Hutterite children whenever I had a chance. Solitary, I tried to imagine what life would be like as part of a flock. The little Hutterite girls gave nothing away. They kept their faces blank under their polka-dotted headscarves, and only their eyes darted here and there.

How the clerks in the dime store or J. C. Penney's sprang to guard their merchandise whenever a cluster of kerchiefed and heavily skirted women and girls from the colony managed to sneak away from their menfolk long enough for an excursion down the forbidden aisles! Jabbering away among themselves like crows, glancing nervously over their shoulders, the Hutterite women fingered the piles of neon-pink and green ankle socks, the garish rayon panties and brassieres, until the shadow of a bearded face through the plate-glass doors sent them flapping. Candy and cosmetics and small, brightly colored objects were likely to disappear with them.

It was said that each of the Hutterites was given a dollar for spending money for their monthly visits to town—"And that's why they can afford new machinery and that walk-in freezer plant at the colony," said my father, contemptuous of such spinelessness. "They'll do without anything the boss or the preacher tells them to do without."

"One of them Hoots told me, *We don't think it's stealing as long as we take it in broad daylight!*" sputtered an indignant merchant.

"Goes to show," somebody was sure to remark, "them Hoot kids would be like any other kids, if they just had the chance. They want the things they see."

What Little Jake must have seen, what Jake wanted, was more seductive than lipstick and colored underwear. *To be a cowboy*—to ride, long-stirruped and obscure, along the crest of the ridge in the chill taupe and gold of late October sundown; to hold, through inch-wide leather reins and a curb bit, the froth of a good horse; to ride by the seat of his pants and the tips of his spurs, in a style as ritualized and aloof as knighthood; to dream of loneliness and of death.

I got spurs that jingle-jangle-jingle . . .

But I won't see my mother
When the work's all done this fall . . .

Next morning just at daybreak
We found where Rocket fell,
Down in a washout forty feet below . . .

I'm ridin' old Paint and leadin' old Dan,
I'm going to Montana to throw a houlihan . . .

They feed in the coulees,
They water in the draws,
Their trails are all matted,
Their backs are all sore . . .

Ride around the little dogies,
Ride around real slow,
For the fiery and the snuffy
Are rarin' to go . . .

Last night as I lay on the prairie
And gazed at the stars in the sky,
I wondered if ever a cowboy
Could go to that sweet by and by . . .

That romantic, despairing tradition of the West had been luring boys away from their homes since the days of Buffalo Bill's Wild West Show, since the first dime novels, perhaps since the *Leatherstocking Tales.* I myself was weeping over *Smoky, the Story of a Cowhorse* at the same time Little Jake was living in his dilemma between the old ways of the Hutterites and the romance of the cowboy. It was a year or so later when my mother nudged me and said, *There! That's Jake!* But I had already invested him with glamour. I watched for him after that: compact, agile, already a little bowlegged, always a little apart from the gawky Hutterite boys or the portly, bearded elders.

Where could a Hutterite boy have learned Jake's natural hand with a bronc? The young men who rode through our place offended my father because they jerked at their horses' mouths and sat their saddles like sacks of meal in their home-made black pants and jackets and clumsy shoes. But whether through aptitude or longing or gradual assimilation into place (in twenty years, all Hutterite boys knew how to ride), Jake handled a horse with the nonchalance of my father and his cousins. He swung down from the saddle like a cowboy, tucking his bridle reins over his arm casually, as though he wouldn't have control instantly if his horse shied suddenly and jerked back. Among men who valued style almost as much as skill, Jake seemed one of them except for his gutturals and his clothes.

By the time I knew Jake by sight, he was breaking horses for ranchers around the county at twenty-five or thirty dollars a head. There was a hot afternoon when I watched through the cracks of the haymow as Jake bucked out a blaze-faced bay in my father's corral. The horse had bogged his head and squealed, bowing his back until the saddle stuck straight up, farting as he landed stiff-legged for eight or ten jolts, until he gave up and stood heaving, dripping foamy sputum around his bit. Jake spurred him and made him trot around the corral. Watching like a voyeur, aware of details I never read about in *Chip, of the Flying U,* I saw how profusely Jake sweated: the glistening rivulets down his forehead, the spreading wet circles under his arms, the wet stains under his crossed suspenders. The suspenders in particular were evidence that I was spying, not just on a man but on an alien one, and I felt a little sickened.

"And you can bet that horse-breaking money of his ain't all going back into the colony," my father remarked.

My mother was unimpressed. "What's he going to do when the big boss finds out?"

For somehow Jake was wearing real Levi's, real cowboy boots, an expensive Stetson hat with his homemade Hutterite shirt and suspenders. Why weren't Hutterites supposed to wear belts? Why did their clothes have to fasten with hooks and eyes? What could possibly be wrong with the buttons on the fly of a pair of Levi's?

"Why doesn't he just leave the Hutterites?" I asked my father.

He answered me so slowly I thought he might have asked himself the same question. "Quitting the colony is harder than you might think."

Then he told me about Big Eli, who had broken so completely with his confession of faith and his pacifism that he enlisted in the army during World War II and fought overseas.

"They say Eli's the best combine man in the country. But when he came home from the army, he couldn't find work. He told me he looked around all the implement dealers and the garages, but as soon as they heard him talk they knew he was a Hutterite, so they wouldn't hire him. He had nowhere to go but back to the colony."

I turned Eli's story over in my mind. It seemed hard that he should be stuck with the bad name of Hutterite when he didn't even want to be one. "Why did he come back here?" I persisted. "Why couldn't he find a place where nobody'd heard of Hutterites?"

But that question had so obvious an answer for my father

that he was surprised I'd even ask. "Guess he just never saw any country he liked near as good as central Montana!"

There was a morning, a few years later, when I hugged a corral post and watched an impromptu sheep-shearing contest between Little Jake and Big Eli—silently rooting, of course, for Jake. Shearing as fast as they could with electric clippers, Eli and Jake kept their teenaged helpers busy dragging up unshorn ewes and hustling off the clipped and dazed. But gradually, fleece by fleece, Jake fell behind Eli's pace. He had been on one of his benders the night before, and his eyes were bloodshot. Good-natured Eli bent over ewe after ewe, peeling off the layers of dirty gray wool with great sweeps of his electrical shearing arm, while Jake poured sweat and blundered with haste, and the helpers grinned, knowing what was going on.

And there was an afternoon when, in my teens, I happened to be walking down Main Street in Lewistown when I saw Jake. He would have been in his late twenties and already badly fallen from grace. He glanced up—would he have recognized me?—and did not quite break his stride. He and I were almost exactly the same height. For half a drawn breath, I looked into bloodshot blue eyes, and then Jake took another step and stumbled off the curb. I heard my mother laughing about it later: *Jake was so busy staring at Mary that he forgot to look where he was going and fell off the sidewalk.*

By that time everyone knew something was wrong with Jake. He had never married, never grew the beard that signified serious Hutterite manhood. His famous benders were beginning to blur together into a soggy alcoholic haze, and stories about his womanizing among the Hutterite women spread far beyond the colony. The Hutterite elders, who had tried to cure his vanity by taking away his hundred-dollar white Stetson, cutting it into inch squares with the tinsnips and returning the pieces to him in a flour sack, must have wondered what remedy to try next. Eventually they remembered the root cellar.

But the drunkenness, the tinsnips, the disgrace and death from cirrhosis were yet to come when, in the late 1940s, we were absorbed in our little range war on the slopes of the South Moccasins and a teenaged Jake rode in one night to say, "Dey're going to be gadderin' cattle in the morning, Jack. You might vant to be lookin' at dere brands."

| | | | | | |

The Weir brothers, Alec and Duff, had been our neighbors on the benchland above the Judith River since before I could remember, and the sight of their team of workhorses and their wagon at our gate, with the two round Scotchmen side by side on the wagon seat, was a rare interruption of our solitude. The Weirs were old bachelors who still spoke with the lilting, almost unintelligible burr of their native crags and heath. Alec was the older. He always held the reins; he always drove the team, just as he looked after their cattle and planned the farming while Duff saw to the housekeeping and cooking.

In their decent brown woolens, the Weirs looked as alike as elderly robins, but Alec was gruffer, more taciturn than Duff. They were more than friends, and the arrival of their wagon, the sight of their round red faces under their cloth caps, meant two extra plates at the supper table and the pleasure of listening to their sweet, perplexing burrs.

Some moments are as permanent as memory; and one of those evenings, or many of those evenings elided into a single glow of a bare electric bulb on oilcloth and the remains of supper—roasted beef and boiled potatoes and thick milk gravy—the roaring security of the wood range, the purple slabs of serviceberry pie being passed around, and the circle of familiar faces at the rim of consciousness, remains as *now, how things are,* including dour, mustached Alec and gentle

Duff as they shovel down their suppers with relish. How can such a moment break into fragments? How can I imagine an alternative *now*? Can I imagine my rugged grandmother— who is just now tramping in from the cow barn carrying two buckets of foaming fresh milk—confined in Duff's clean, cur- tainless little kitchen, where the only milk is in the can of Carnation?

The *midnights* loom up along the horizon, riders in black, their shadows darkening the grass, even the bays and browns of their horses blackening in the sharp wind, and only a shirt here and there in dark green or rust, with the faces of the riders pinkish with cold, their noses watering from the wind. Are they substantial, or an image out of something I read?

Alec Weir rides toward the crest of the hill. His horse's hooves echo on the frozen dirt track. The air grows colder as he rides out of the gully and emerges from the bare black branches of hawthorns and chokecherries into the undeflected wind on the slope that leads higher into the bluish-dark stain of pines. No movement in the empty, heavily grazed grass. Not a magpie flaps across that gray snow-laden sky, not a calf bawls, though the signs of cattle are plentiful on the trail and scattered through the bunchgrass.

Where are his missing cattle? Alec rides heavily. He is not a young man, and he has never sat easily, naturally in a saddle, but he knows the country and his eyes are alert for any signs of life. Whether or not the Hutterites really are cattle thieves, Alec has believed the warning carried by the boy, Little Jake.

| | | | | | |

What happened to Alec? Did he come upon the makeshift corral, hidden in the pines? The glint of red hide and white faces, the walleyed calves peering through the unpeeled poles, his thirty missing head? Did he catch sight of the men who drove them there, and did one of them react in haste?

Or—no cattle, no dark riders, just a misstep on a familiar trail—did his gentle old horse catch him unawares when it stumbled and fell? In this episode, as in so many, the evidence is inconclusive. When his horse came back to the barn without him, muddied down its flank and side from its fall, Duff started to search and found his brother facedown at the bottom of the coulee.

"Poor old man," said my mother, much later. "I suppose he tried to scramble out from under his horse, but he just wasn't quick enough."

| | | | | | |

Weir cattle were found in a Hutterite corral that fall; whether by accident or by a clumsy attempt at cattle rustling was never determined. Duff Weir did not have the spirit to bring charges. The rumor that Alec's body had been robbed of the substantial amount of cash he was believed always to have carried remained rumor. Heartbroken, Duff sold the ranch and moved to town.

But for the rest of the time we lived next to the colony, my father rode and checked brands. One chill November morning I sat on a pony and watched as he and Joe Murray heeled and headed a shaggy yearling calf and stretched it out between their saddle horses to clip its flank and look for evidence that its brand had been altered. With a gloved hand my father brushed away the clumps of rusty hair where Joe had clipped and looked at the bare patch of hide for a long time, but at last he shook his head. Nothing conclusive was ever going to vindicate Little Jake or give meaning to Alec Weir's death.

Joe Murray went to work again with the hand clippers on the calf's thick winter coat, clipping large block letters that spread across its whole side and could be seen for miles: HOOT.

Then he and my father mounted their horses and loosened their lariats. We all watched as the calf struggled to its feet and trotted off toward the pines, emblazoned with its legend. It was a last word of sorts.

| | | | | | |

While Jake turned to booze, I turned to books and found in them something like the solace of the heavy red wine the Hutterites vinted from chokecherries and also some of its sour smack. The *midnights*, I came to understand, had risen out of my dreams and from nowhere else. The Hutterite boys were only boys, boys who finally learned cowboy skills, though only Jake, I think, became a cowboy.

AUNTIE

Jack Hogeland with Socks and Babe, 1937.

||||||||||||||||||||||||||||||||||||||||||||||||||

Summer of 1942. The boys have gone overseas, but the war still seems remote, and the long afternoons stretch as interminably, as unlikely to change, as the slow hooves of the workhorses. Tires and gasoline are rationed now, and along the Judith River in central Montana the hay is being mowed and bucked and stacked in the old way, with teams of horses. Horses have furnished the heavy power for haying here for fifty years, and horses will plod ahead of the buck rakes and hay wagons for a few more years, when the end of the war will release tractors and heavy machinery to the implement dealers.

But I am not yet three years old in the summer of 1942, and my first fragments of memories are as unpredictable as the future.

The sun glares on the whitened alkali road outside the log house. When I climb into Auntie's Ford sedan, its gray plush upholstery scratches my face. Beyond its wide open doors, the scents and sounds of June are seamless, without beginning or end—warm sweet clover and mown hay, sickle oil and the snap of grasshoppers and the purposeful voices of adults—

but the car contains its own smell of dust and dread. I hate the scratchy upholstery. But when I stand up on it, I am tall enough to see over the back of the front seat.

Auntie is propped in the back seat with her feet up. Her braids are pinned around her head, and she still wears the Levi's and the white shirt, gray now with hayfield dust and sweat, that she put on this morning when she went out to mow the lower meadow with the sorrel team. I cannot see her foot under the wrapping of towels, but I can smell a darker secretion than sweat.

Auntie recognizes me.

"Look what they did to me, Mary." And she laughs. Her laugh is like summer, like Auntie.

But adult hands suddenly lift me from the front seat of the car and set me down in the white blaze of sunlight.

| | | | | | | |

The next time I see my aunt Imogene, she wears a sunken white line like a slave bracelet all the way around her right ankle. I am seven now and, with a child's callused certainty that all stories end well, I know but don't care that she nearly lost her foot in a mowing accident, nearly bled to death, that all that saved her was her own level head in stopping the runaway team and taking off her belt and twisting it around her ankle for a tourniquet. Auntie is Auntie. Nothing can happen to her. She is summer. Her laugh rolls at practically anything.

My little sister, Betty, and I have never been to school. We are living on the old home ranch at the mouth of Spring Creek, miles from any school over treacherous gumbo roads, and we are wild for a playmate. We shriek and throw ourselves on Auntie when she arrives.

"Now I know why Aunt Mable used to gasp when I jumped

in her lap," she complains. "Look at the bruises you've left on me!"

"Not my elbow size," I say, measuring my elbow on the bruise.

"Not my elbow size," Betty says, doing the same.

"No, but it's somebody's knee size," says Auntie. But she laughs all the same.

After her school term ends in June, she shows up at the ranch for long weeks of helping with the garden, canning, butchering chickens, playing with us, wading in the creek, so familiar a part of the household that she automatically snatches the doll dress off the cat as he dashes for the open kitchen door and the peace and quiet of the corrals. But she doesn't help with the haying. The war is over and the boys have come home. My big cousin Joe Murray is home from the navy and working for my father, and the corrals and sheds and hayfields are held by the deeper rhythms of male voices and the clink of wrenches on machinery being repaired for the season.

Instead, Auntie is going to teach Betty and me how to swim.

Every afternoon after the dinner dishes are done, carrying towels, we walk with Auntie up through the garden, along the rows of peas and leaf lettuce and corn on our shortcut to the lane. Sometimes the cat follows as far as the fence before he slips off on his own business. Betty and I roll under the lowest strand of barbed wire while Auntie makes a handful of the top wires and swings her leg over in the awkward, careful way of adults. The moment is one of the few times we remember that she is not a child, that in another life she is a high school teacher in a faraway place called Port Angeles, Washington.

Betty and I have never been out of central Montana. Behind us the bare shale hills and exposed sagebrush and cutbanks stretch up toward the slopes of the South Moccasin Mountains, but the two ruts of the lane lead across our slough, pockmarked by the deep hoofprints of the milk cows, down into the dark green shade of chokecherries and grass and the supple golden willows that crisscross their narrow leaves over the dazzle of running water. Spring Creek.

In our underpants, white-legged and uneasy, our clothes in two small heaps on the gravel bar behind us, Betty and I balk at the wet brown brink.

Up to her waist in the easy current, Auntie coaxes us. "Come on! You can't learn to swim if you won't get wet!"

"It's cold!"

"It's not cold!"

To show us, she submerges to the neck and swims a few strokes to the other side of the swimming hole. Through the reflection of the willows, in her black suit and white rubber cap, she looks alien and competent. But we still won't venture in. How can we be other than afraid? We are little dryland girls. The most water we've ever seen is the Judith River, which we've been told to stay away from. We don't even take baths in anything bigger than a galvanized tub.

Finally, while Betty plays in the mud and pebbles along the bank, Auntie manages to persuade me into waist-deep water. With a hand under my back and one under my head, she tries to teach me to float. As long as I can feel her hands supporting me, I can lie back and relax, but when I feel myself being drawn downstream, a part of the current, I panic and thrash.

"You were floating! Couldn't you feel it?"

"The current!" I sputter, bobbing up and feeling the reassurance of gravel under my toes.

"I won't let you float beyond the length of my arm! I promise!"

But I don't trust her. Although she is older than my mother, Auntie is not quite an adult. Not a parent. When I tip back with the water rising in my hair and rippling over my ears, the sun shooting red bursts against my eyelids through the willow leaves, the hands under my back are as insubstantial as the air. When I feel the current take me, I panic. It will be years before I learn to swim. As for Betty, all that summer she refuses to wade in water deeper than her toes.

My mother is busy as always with her chickens and garden and freezing and canning and the extra cooking during haying season. She's never had time to take us to the creek, and she won't let us play there alone. When we burst into the kitchen, she looks up from her dishpan, where she is rinsing spinach, with eyes as vague as though she doesn't recognize us.

When we drag her back from whatever she's been dreaming about, she doesn't seem surprised that we aren't learning to swim.

"You should have seen Auntie trying to learn to swim in an irrigation ditch," she says.

Auntie giggles.

"What? What? Tell us about it!" we demand.

"I knew I was going to have to take swimming in college, and I was trying to learn to float. The irrigation ditch was the only water I had to practice in. Just as I'd lie back, *plop!*"

They are both laughing.

"Your mother and your uncle David were running along the bank and throwing frogs at me," Auntie explains.

Betty and I stare at our stern mother, trying to believe she ever did anything as frivolous as throwing frogs. If anyone is an adult, it is our mother. She never wastes time, rarely does anything for pleasure. Impossible to believe that she is Auntie's younger sister—Auntie who has her hair done in a beauty shop in mysterious Port Angeles; Auntie who smokes cigarettes.

"Imogene's almost as big a kid as the girls are," we have heard our mother remark, and we understand she is not praising her.

It is this summer, or perhaps the next (for my mother's

remarks, repeated with small variations to Grammy over the cream separator or over the buckets of peas she is shelling, at family picnics or around the supper table, have the tendency to blur into a single pronouncement), that I become aware of her interdiction: *I don't think Imogene's ever going to get married.*

Gradually the interdiction becomes more global: *Some people just aren't meant to get married.*

"There's always one old maid in every generation in our family," she explains to Grammy. "There's my aunt Mable and now Imogene."

| | | | | | | |

Haying season in these first years after the war comes with its own frantic, festive ritual. Haying season is the men. It is a water bottle clinking with diminishing ice, coated with bits of leaf and grass and fine pulverized dust in its shady uncut corner of the meadow. A shower of sparks and a shriek from the grinder from the log shed where my father is sharpening sickles. Meals of cold fried chicken and potato salad thrown on the table by my mother, who has dashed in from a day on the buck rake. But haying season belongs to the men. Their dirty slanted Stetsons and grimed faces, white teeth and hand-rolled cigarettes. The texture of their voices, the way their Levi's fit, the way they ride the mowers with their legs braced and their gloved hands full of lines. Their glamour.

Although the whole family turns out for haying. Grammy drives the stacker team. She walks all day behind old Bess and Bally with their hooves as big as dinner plates, plodding back and forth while the teeth of the stacker rise to the top of the stack with the load of hay and come down empty. Old Bill Hafer builds the stack. He's up on top with a pitchfork, meeting the load. Years from now, in a university literature class, I will be assigned Robert Frost for the first time and in a burst of pleasure understand that Bill *bundles every forkful in its place, and tags and numbers it for future reference.* But that will be in another life, one I don't yet dream of. Haying season is now, forever. I tear around on one of the ponies, carrying messages, getting in the way.

Small Theo, who is putting up his own hay across the river, has bought himself a fancy new hay baler, but my father swears by loose hay and the old ways of haying. He won't change willingly.

He mows the meadows with his fast sorrel team, a half a day ahead of Joe Murray and the swather. The sickle bar follows the mower, six inches off the ground; its razor teeth of sharpened sickles flatten the heavy wild grasses, the bobbing seed heads. I have to be warned again and again to keep away.

None of the other teams can keep up with my father and the sorrels. The sorrels aren't colts anymore, but they prance at the end of a hard day. A classy pair at a time when men took pride in the looks and the close match of their teams, the sorrels are crossbred shire horse and saddle stock, a little smaller than the other teams but ready for anything. Babe, the mare, is a hand taller than Socks, the gelding, but he is heavily muscled and powerful. His four white legs and his white bald face draw the eye. He is the spooky one of the pair, although Babe is always ready to run with him.

Joe Murray helped break the sorrels, before the war. Joe's scare was one of the men's stories, endlessly repeated around the supper table or on Sunday afternoons. How I loved to hear their talk, to hear how my father had hitched up the flashy red colts with a W! He handed the end of the rope on the W to Joe, then a kid of fifteen, just out from town for the summer. "Pull this when they start to run," he said.

"Hell, I didn't know a goddamn thing." Joe always told his part of the story. "I got in the wagon with him."

Then Socks plunged and Babe plunged with him. As the wagon shot off the road into sagebrush Joe panicked and jumped out the endgate. He was still holding the rope. He had no idea what pulling on it would do. Jerked along by his arms, he finally found out. The rope, threaded through a surcingle to straps around the colts' front feet, formed the shape of a W which contracted and spilled them, crashing, midgallop.

My father broke scores of colts to harness during the 1930s. No one had any money to pay for horse breaking. He broke work teams quickly in exchange for the use of them, with a W. Being spilled on their knees and noses once or twice will persuade most colts to obey the curb of the lines, but the sorrels never got over their urge to run. They became notorious.

Several of their runs were epic, told and retold whenever the men got together. Like the time they stampeded for several miles over river cutbanks, across shallows and deep holes, and through fences on the other side of the river with Joe's younger brother Ted careening in the wagon behind them, able to do nothing but hang on. But when they finally stopped on their own, heaving for breath, Ted turned them in a rage and drove them all the miles back in their own tracks. ("And I *seen* some of the hills they'd run up and he'd run them down, and I couldn't see *how* in the hell he done it—")

I hung on the back of my father's chair, listening. I preferred the men's stories; they were much more thrilling, more fully narrated and action-packed, than the elliptical, encoded talk of the women. (One simple, elementary difficulty with the women's talk took me years to comprehend. What they wanted to talk about couldn't be discussed in front of children.)

| | | | | | |

And then there was the time in 1942 when the sorrel team ran away with Imogene and nearly killed her.

The boys were overseas; ranch help was scarce. Imogene had finished her school term and had come to help with the haying. She was mowing alone on the lower meadow. My father was working a quarter of a mile away. I can imagine clearly how it must have been, that afternoon. One minute all movement in the drowsy June heat was predictable, slow, unchangeable. The next minute everything had changed. The sorrels started at something, nothing, in the foolish way of horses, and stampeded. Somehow or other the sickle bar passed over Imogene's foot, those gleaming four-inch razor teeth slicing in the split of a second to the bone.

At some point my father glanced across the wash and noticed she hadn't made another round with the mower. Then he spotted the sorrels standing in the fence corner, and he unhitched one of his own horses and jumped on her bareback and galloped the quarter of a mile. By the time he reached her, Imogene had tied up the team and was twisting her belt around her ankle. My father assessed the depth of the cut and kicked the workhorse into a run for the house, counting ration points in his head, calculating the few gallons of gas they had on the place against the thirty miles to the hospital in Lewistown. He and my mother propped Imogene in the back seat of her own car and tore off for town, leaving me screaming with Grammy. Betty was five months from being born.

None of them thought the foot could be saved. Imogene, fully conscious, knew for the whole of the thirty-mile, hour-long drive over alkali dust and potholed gravel that if her foot was amputated, she would never get another teaching job. She would never again be self-supporting. One minute her life had been as unchangeable as the drowse of insects in the high grass ahead of the sickle bar, predictable as the flick of a horse's tail at a fly. The next minute everything had changed.

| | | | | | | |

Graduating from Denton High School in 1927, she really had had no choice. Teaching in the far-flung rural schools was the one certain road to marginal independence for young women. Even in the bad drought years of the twenties, every penniless, windblown, dried-out community maintained its one-room school for anywhere from five to twenty-five pupils spread out in the eight grades. Every school required a teacher willing and able to carry her own coal and start her own fire every morning in thirty-below-zero weather, to sweep out the school and carry in her own water and wash the blackboard and invent lessons with no school supplies, to shovel paths through the snow to the boys' and girls' outhouses and out to the barn where the pupils unhitched their buggy horses or tied their saddle horses during the day, to join in their games at recess and go down to the barn with them after school and help the youngest ones hitch up, to live in a one-room teacherage behind the school with a kerosene lamp and a bucket of spring water and no refrigeration, to hope to get to town perhaps once or twice during a winter—all for something less than a hundred dollars a month, supposing the community had the money to honor its pay warrants.

Imogene's mother, my grandmother Welch, taught in dozens of rural schools scattered across Fergus County and Judith Basin County, a year here, a year there. She managed to scrape the money out of her salary to send all three of her daughters for teacher training. She was giving her girls their chance to stand on their own feet and marry from choice. Imogene spent the last years of the 1920s at the state normal school that later would become Western Montana College at Dillon, and then she was on her own. She was eighteen.

"Ma gave me a lot of advice we didn't get in teacher-training courses," she said. "One thing she told me was always to go down to the barn and stay there until every kid had saddled or hitched his horse and started for home. I was down at the barn the afternoon one of the boys decided to ride his horse into the schoolhouse. Right across that rotten old floor. I don't know why he and the horse didn't fall through it and break both their necks."

Most of those one-room schools have vanished since Imogene and my mother and grandmother taught in them, closed because of better rural roads and consolidated schools, a shrinking ranch population, and the unwillingness of teachers to labor under the old conditions. Of the hundred-odd rural schools in Fergus County in the 1920s, six were still open in 1988, and four of them were located on Hutterite colonies.

One more piece of the vanishing countryside. With the rural schools have vanished those armies of women of all ages in their dark rayon print dresses, heavy from their starchy diets, graying as the years passed, weather-beaten and cranky, moving from school to school, year by year, in their tenureless quest for a bare living, for an independence of sorts.

My mother taught for two years at the Conard school. She already knew she wanted no part of her mother's endless trek from school to school, of the yeast smells of teacherages where women lived alone, of the unrelenting female life. She liked the family she boarded with, though. They were the Conards. They took her along on Sundays when they visited at the Theo Hogeland ranch on Warm Spring Creek.

Theo Hogeland, and his wife, Em, were famous for their hospitality. Em never knew if she'd be feeding two or twenty at Sunday dinner. Neighbors, cousins, cowboys, strangers, all were welcome. Theo's great-nephew, Jack, was running a trapline on the lower Judith that winter and helping his uncle Theo winter a band of sheep. Barely in his twenties, Jack and his mother had a little ranch of their own on the south slope of the South Moccasins. Seeing Jack for the first time as he rode down from the bluffs on his snuffy saddle horse to Uncle Theo's for Sunday dinner, the young teacher must have been struck at once by his cowboy glamour. She told her mother she was done with teaching.

But for Imogene with the ready laugh, with the thick curly hair wound in its braid around her head, there were one or two boyfriends but never one who presented himself seriously enough to take focus.

"Never thought much of that old Lud she was going with," sniffed my mother.

Lud? Whoever he was, he did Imogene one favor while she was living in the teacherage at the Roy school.

To be eighteen or nineteen or twenty and living alone in one of those remote schools at a time when distance had not yet shrunk and telephones were nonexistent, when ten miles meant an hour or more by buggy or saddle horse, when outward standards of decorum and morality were one thing and community practice was another, brought some of the young teachers to an edge of another kind.

Lud brought Imogene a gift of a .22 rifle and spent a Sunday afternoon taking turns with her, pinging at tin cans. When she went to gather up the cans, he said, "Leave 'em lay. Some people may as well know you got a gun and you can shoot it."

That night, when the young men finally worked up their nerve and approached the teacherage, Imogene blew out her lamp and fastened the flimsy door. In the dark, in her haste, she jammed the .22. She knew, from what the eighth-grade girls had let drop, what had happened to the last teacher. Through the door, alone in the dark, she listened to the boys' boozy boasts.

Then they started talking about the tin cans.

"Hell, she's got a gun."

Perhaps it was the excuse they needed to back off. At any rate, they left her alone.

"But what about the last teacher? What did people in the community say?" I demanded, aghast, when Imogene told me the story years later.

"One old man said, *Hell, them boys don't get to town very often.* And then she got to marry one of them."

"Was rape a common threat in the teacherages?"

Imogene thought back. "I knew of one teacher who was raped. She was at the Hilger school. Ma knew about it, and so did the superintendent of schools, because I overheard them talking about it. But they would never have discussed it in front of us unmarried girls."

"Didn't they warn you? Weren't they concerned about your safety, for God's sake?"

"Well . . ." Imogene was half defensive, half apologetic for the summary ways of her generation. "That was in the teacherages. When your mother and I started out, we always boarded, so we weren't alone."

| | | | | | | |

Such was the life Imogene faced losing, that afternoon in June of 1942 when she lay in the back seat of her little Ford and watched the road through the sagebrush of the lower Judith gradually rise into blue mountain slopes and creek meadows and cottonwoods while her young brother-in-law drove as fast as he dared on dubious tires over the potholed gravel road to Lewistown.

But in tiny St. Joseph's Hospital, at the top of the Main Street hill, Dr. Solterro and Sister St. Paul met the car and carried her into the operating room and went to work with sutures. Imogene woke up the next morning in one of the narrow white rooms overlooking the nuns' chicken yard and knew she still had her foot.

"But I was on crutches for a year. Everybody in Fergus

County had heard about it. School boards wouldn't *look* at me. So I sent out applications to parts of the world where nobody knew me."

In 1942 the shipyards of the Pacific Northwest were running at top capacity, around the clock, back-to-back shifts, insatiable for labor. In Seattle and Tacoma, Bremerton and Bellingham, women were leaving their teaching jobs and signing on for the big hourly wages at the yards. Suddenly teachers were scarce. School districts became frantic. A woman from Montana on crutches? At least she wouldn't be lured away by the shipyards.

Imogene mailed her applications to towns she had never heard of, towns with names that sounded of rain forests and tides—Anacortes, Mukilteo, Port Townsend, Port Angeles. When she hobbled out to the mailbox on the county road, she found a handful of replies. In September she loaded her Ford, stuck her crutches in the seat beside her, and drove west alone.

| | | | | | |

For Betty and me she became the monthly letter addressed to my mother, letters that eventually were addressed to us. With birthday checks enclosed. The extravagant packages at Christmas, the dolls bought in Seattle. And showing up again regularly at the ranch in June, she became Auntie of summer. We were the luckiest of little girls. To be loved by your mother's sister is to have a second, unconditional mother. Because she is powerless, she cannot curb you; because she has nothing at stake, because she will reap none of the blame for what you turn out to be, she can love and love and never criticize, never question, never judge.

| | | | | | |

"I wonder what Imogene thinks she's doing out there."

"She's bought a *Buick?*"

"Her own house? What does a single woman want with her own house?"

| | | | | | | |

A year after Imogene left Montana, another bolt struck my mother's family. Her parents had been living in the teacherage at the Straw school, where my grandmother Welch happened to be teaching that year. She was the family mainstay. My grandfather, a failed homesteader, a failed insurance salesman, had grown dimmer and more incompetent over the years. Little was expected of him, and he seemed to expect little. Harmless, growing a little bizarre in his behavior—how bizarre, no one but my grandmother knew. Late one night a message was relayed by the postmaster at Danvers, who had a telephone, to Small Theo on his side of the Judith River, who saddled a horse and rode across the river to let my mother and father know that my grandmother had walked to the grain elevator at Straw and woken the manager to use his telephone and send word that she needed help.

Betty and I, sleeping through the alarm, knew nothing of my grandfather's breakdown. We woke the next morning to find ourselves in the charge of Grammy. No one wanted to tell us what was happening. It took me months of eavesdropping, stringing together stolen snips of conversation, to learn that our parents had dressed and driven to Straw in the middle of the night and found my grandfather in a peculiar state. Rational one minute, shivering with fright or rage the next, he harbored the notion that my grandmother was plotting to kill him.

The voices weave themselves from fragments:

"He set there in the hospital room and visited with me,

just the same as he ever did—you'd never known nothing was wrong until *she* come in, then he's shaking all over and trying to climb out the window. She can't take care of him any longer. Hell, she's the one person that can't take care of him."

"We can't have him here!" my mother flashes. "I can't have him here with the girls!"

My grandmother Welch, that indomitable old woman, refused to lay down the burden of responsibility that had been increasingly hers for years. She would not lay it on one of her daughters. She would see to my grandfather's care, if not personally, then financially. A private nursing home, very well. By living marginally herself, she could pay the annual fee. She could pay it, at least, as long as she went on teaching. She was nearly seventy.

For all my eavesdropping, I knew nothing of the financial yoke around her neck. I knew from listening that my grandmother was worried about the mandatory retirement age, set at that time at seventy, for teachers in Montana. When she went back to the Iowa of her girlhood to keep house for her widowed brother, one of the reasons was that she could get a country school and teach there until she was seventy-five. I supposed she did it because she liked to teach.

Eventually, of course, my grandfather died. His passing stirred the briefest of family flurries. He was buried in the old Denton cemetery, and at his funeral my sister and I sat between my grandmother Welch, stoical as always, and my mother, who fumed with all the old awakened resentments of her girlhood. Other members of the family must have attended, but I remember only the two women: my dry-eyed grandmother, no more alone than she had been for years, and my mother, whom she had failed to make into a teacher.

| | | | | | |

And the young woman who took her first deep breath of salt air in Port Angeles? What else was she doing, when she wasn't writing loving letters to her nieces and sending presents and coming back to Montana in the summers to try to teach them how to swim?

| | | | | | |

"Ma was in her seventies," Imogene wrote me about the nightmare in Straw when my grandfather broke down. "She could expect no help from your parents. They had Grammy and Bill Hafer to see through their final years. Her other children were struggling to get along. I was teaching in Port Angeles when Ma had a talk with me. If she died before my father, would I take over his care?

"I offered to start paying half his expenses right away. She refused. As long as she lived, could work, she could manage. But if she should die first . . .

"I faced the fact. It would mean I couldn't afford to marry as long as he lived. But I gave her my word. Relieved, she took up her burden. But she never forgot.

"An aunt wanted to see me married. She criticized me for being single. Ma looked at her sister. Spoke. *Don't criticize Imogene to me. She has been a daughter and son both to me.* No more said."

| | | | | | |

I tip back, and water rises in my hair and ripples over my ears. The sun shoots red bursts against my eyelids through the willow leaves, and the hands under my back are as insubstantial as the air. I feel the current take me; I am launched before I realize what has happened. One moment nothing will ever change, the next moment all has changed.

I know now what it is to wear a financial yoke. How could I not have trusted the hands that supported me in the easy current of Spring Creek? Perhaps, after all, I did. Over the babble of waters I hear Auntie's laugh, the laugh of eternal summer.

GETTING
MARRIED

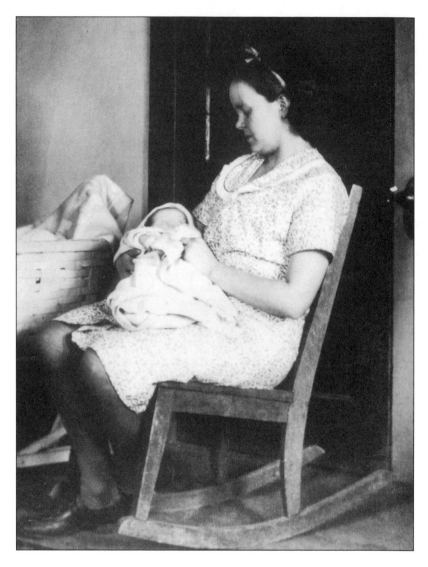

Doris Hogeland with Mary, 1940.

$\mathcal{U}$ncle Theo senior, who later said he could have walked all the way from Lewistown on the carcasses of frozen cattle after the terrible winter of 1887, was a younger brother of Abraham's who had followed him to Montana and filed on his own homestead several miles south of his brother's in a deep cleft in the benchlands where the creek widened its bed and lazed through sixty acres of sheltered bottoms. Here in the shadow of the cleft Theo cleared brush and built his house and corrals and sheepsheds, fenced his hay meadows and home pastures, and planted orchards. He and his wife, Em, threw their house open to the countryside; beds were spread on the floor and in the bunkhouse for young people coming home from the Saturday night dances, and places at the table were set for all passersby. It was at one of their Sunday dinners that my mother met my father.

The road to Theo's led along the side of the hill and into the shade of maples, where the sun receded in the late afternoons and the air stayed temperate from the warm springs in the creek. Such ease must have widened the eyes of a girl from the prairies north of Denton, where not a tree grew to break the wind that drove temperatures down to fifty below zero in winter and scorched every drop of moisture in summer. Brought up to frugality, she looked askance at the bowls of garden vegetables and potatoes and gravy passed around Em's table, the endless roasts of beef or mutton, the pans of light rolls or loaves of bread or fruit pies drawn from the oven of the wood range.

"If Uncle Theo hadn't given away so many groceries, he wouldn't have died so poor," she complained later.

But she was glad enough, at the end of a week of teaching, to sweep out her school and close the windows and ride in the back seat of the Conards' Model T down that precipitous road to the small white house under the spreading maple that had begun life in Pennsylvania as a sapling and had been nourished through those first Montana winters by the man and woman the whole of Fergus County called Uncle Theo and Aunt Em. Anybody was likely to turn up there: the Conards and all their daughters and their daughters' young men; cowboys and cousins from up and down the Judith; Archie Merriweather with his banjo, Jess Sample riding in from Theo's sheep camp, old Frenchy Pernot shambling out his last days in Theo's bunkhouse.

When Archie looked around Em's table one night and counted, "Fifteen human beings and one schoolteacher!" my mother laughed as hard as anyone. She was twenty-one.

Sometimes I could get her to describe the winter dances of the 1930s, when she and my father and the Conard girls and their beaux would ride horseback for miles through all kinds of weather to dance in a school or a community hall until the kerosene lanterns swayed on their hooks to the music of an untuned piano or a fiddle and Archie's banjo. At midnight everybody would stop dancing for a supper of sandwiches and cake and coffee, then dance again until three or four or five o'clock in the morning, then ride back through blowing snow to Uncle Theo's to help him do his morning chores, milk his cows, eat breakfast, and go to bed.

"Why don't you go to dances now?" I asked her when I was old enough to look forward to going myself.

"We're getting too old, I guess."

Courtship for my father had meant long night rides on Pardner to Uncle Theo's to meet my mother. I knew, because he told me, about the songs he sang as he rode alone and out of earshot of the world.

Old Faithful, we rode the range together.

Old Faithful, in every kind of weather . . .
There's a coyote howling to the moon above,
So carry me back to the one I love . . .

When I was ten, I was intensely curious about that courtship, but it was hard to dig details out of my mother.

"When did you first find out they were in love?" I asked Grammy.

She obligingly rummaged back through her recollections. "Well, I remember Jack coming home from Uncle Theo's one night and telling me that the schoolteacher at the Conards' was just a kid . . ."

After their marriage, they moved into the log house on the lower Judith with Grammy and Bill Hafer. The water reeked of alkali, and the mice were so bad they kept their food in a tin-lined wooden crate they called the Grub Box. Finally her father gave her a cat named Florence, but my mother said she got to be almost as quick as the cat at catching mice.

Depression had settled into Montana on top of the drought that had already blighted the land, and bore down even upon the young homestead-born like my mother and father who had come of age without expectations. Her parents had been among those who lost their savings when over half of Montana's commercial banks failed during the 1920s, among the half of all Montana farmers who lost their land. The thirties promised to be more of the same. In the crippled mining and smelter towns of Butte and Anaconda, Great Falls and East Helena, in the little plains communities of Scobey and Broadus and Jordan, Glasgow and Plentywood, families were going hungry. The Red Cross came into eastern Montana and doled out food and fuel. Nobody expected to see cash from one month to the next.

During the first of the drought years Uncle Theo and Aunt Em tried to succor their neighbors, as they always had. When pastureland shriveled and cattle starved, when men turned out their sheep along the roads because they couldn't afford to feed them and shear their worthless pelts, when the drought and grasshoppers descended into his sheltered creek bottom, Uncle Theo tried turkeys. He encouraged everybody to buy day-old birds and herd them in the dried-out wheat fields, where they ate the weeds and the grasshoppers but had to be guarded day and night against the coyotes. When the flocks were ready to be butchered, he got his neighbors together again to pluck and dress their birds and haul them by truck to Danvers where they could be shipped by rail to markets suddenly overwhelmed by too many fresh turkeys.

He could help his neighbors no longer; he could hardly help himself. For Uncle Theo, who had created a garden of apples and gooseberries and gladioli out of a brushy creek bottom, who had organized a school district and built the first schoolhouse at Huson's dipping tank, pressing his brother Abraham into service as its teacher, who had founded the county 4-H clubs and served on the original Fergus County Fair Board, now bereft of the luxuries of community service and charity, the depression was truly the Great Leveler.

As years passed, my father invested the thirties with the

virtues of austerity. "We didn't have much, but then we didn't need much," he always told us. "We lived the way the old-timers always had, and we got along. We didn't have electricity, so we didn't have a light bill. We used horses for work. We couldn't afford to keep license plates on a car. Some people used to muddy up an old set of license plates, or borrow a neighbor's plates if they had to go to town. We all knew how to be neighbors."

My mother's infrequent stories, however, were bare of romance. "The chickens were laying good the summer after we were married. We couldn't sell the eggs for enough to pay for the gas to haul them to town, so we ate eggs, every day, all summer. Fried for breakfast, hard-boiled for dinner, scrambled for supper. Bill Hafer would come in and see eggs on the table again, and his face would fall."

Then, always: *You kids don't know what it is to do without!*

That was a clue of sorts, I came to believe, for her disdain. I could never know what she knew.

Nor could I know her. For my mother was never a child. She had materialized, larger than life in her starched house-dress, the day I slipped while climbing the wire gate and hung by my hand from a barb until I tore loose and fell. I was not three years old, but I carry the scar in my palm to this day, a tiny white line that diverges in a Y, and I carry that first memory of the woman who scooped me out of the dirt and bore me into the log house, scolding: "Can't you ever walk through a gate? Why do you always have to climb?"

| | | | | | | |

Later, when my aunts told stories about my mother as a child, I could never quite believe in them. And my mother hated to hear them. A holiday dinner once was destroyed when her older sisters, Sylva and Imogene, began to reminisce about the time they had been hauling drinking water in a barrel in the back of a wagon. Perhaps their well had gone dry; at any rate, the family had had to resort to hauling water from a spring several miles away, and once they got the water home, they had to bail it in a bucket from the barrel on the wagon to a barrel on the ground.

"There was Doris on the wagon, bailing water with that rusty old bucket Ma used to feed the pigs. *Doris, whatever possessed you to ruin the drinking water with that awful old bucket?* Ma asked her, and Doris said, *It wasn't my fault! Sylva let me do it!*"

My mother flung down her fork. Everybody who hadn't paid much attention to the story thus far looked up with apprehension. "It *wasn't* my fault! How was I to know I wasn't supposed to use that bucket?"

"You were fourteen—" began her sister Sylva, unwisely.

"I always got the blame! From all of you! And you were all older than me! It wasn't my fault!"

To my astonishment, my mother was crying.

"Jesus Christ!" said my father, slamming down his cup. "Can't anybody in your family forget anything? I don't ever want to hear another goddamned word about that goddamned bucket and that barrel of water!"

Silence ended that dinner, and neither of my aunts ever, ever mentioned the barrel of water and the rusty bucket in my mother's or my father's presence again.

"What was she like when she was my age?" I probed.

"She and your uncle Dave fought so hard at the supper table that Ma kept a wooden spoon by her plate to rap their heads with," Imogene told me.

"One time she cut up the dish towels to make doll clothes," said my grandmother Welch. "She'd kept after me, *Ma, can I do this? Can I do that?* till I said yes, yes, without really paying attention. Next thing I knew—"

My mother didn't like that story, either. "It was Ma's own

fault!" she flashed. "When we moved to the teacherage, she didn't take along any cloth for me to sew on. She should have known that I'd need something to do. But she never cared about me."

When descriptions frayed into anecdotes, I fell back on snapshots. Today I pore over those same snapshots with no more sense of finding my mother than I had when I was ten. In a handful of these pictures she is a small girl in a picot dress kept white and ironed at incalculable cost, her hair cut straight across her forehead, posed against the blistered siding of the two-room house on the homestead. In another she is twelve or thirteen, and she sits on a crate by a barbed-wire fence. Her hair, cut in the same bob, falls about her face as she rinses out a garment in a basin. Her small, strong hands are familiar, and her slim legs. Also familiar is the background: the absence of shade, the fence fading off interminably, the weeds.

Now her hair is waved about her face. She is living in Billings, attending normal school for a year and a half until she can get her teaching certificate, and her chin juts out when she smiles. She likes Billings, she likes her roommates, but classes are a bore and she'll be glad to be done with them.

And now, just a year or two later, she stands with my father on the steps of the Methodist parsonage in Denton just after their wedding ceremony. She wears a new crepe dress and white shoes, and she carries a sheaf of flowers, and my father wears a stiff new suit. Her parents and Grammy and Uncle Theo and Aunt Em pose with them, and she flashes her wide smile.

"They look so happy," said my sister as we sorted through the family pictures, and I agreed, jarred by the obvious. Because my mother always seemed so unhappy.

Another snapshot, a shadowy interior of bare walls and bare floor like a documentary of the Dust Bowl. I know the date is 1940 because I am the month-old infant lying on my mother's lap. She sits in a wooden rocking chair, in profile, her eyes on me. I can almost see the years settling in, the web of lines contracting her face. She has gained perhaps fifty pounds since her wedding day.

She had expected hard work after her marriage, and doing without; she had been brought up to both. She did the wash for herself and my father, Grammy and Bill, and one or more of the Murray boys, who stayed out on the ranch with them during the summers; it meant carrying every sheet and pillowcase, shirt and pair of Levi's down to the river to scrub on a board. The alkali from the well ate holes in the clothes and stained the sheets yellow.

"Don't wash out her diapers every time," her mother advised her when I was born, "not if she's just wet them. You'll save so much work if you hang them up and let them dry and use them again."

Getting married meant doing the work she had been brought up to in an unfamiliar context. She didn't like Grammy's starchy cooking; she gradually took over the kitchen and planted a garden and coaxed my father to eat fresh green peas and snap beans. And she felt uneasy around the Hogelands, with their big ideas about themselves. She couldn't get used to living on credit and hoping to break even when the cattle were sold in the fall. Her own mother had banked her pay warrants at the end of every month and laid down cash for every sack of flour and sugar she carried home.

"They told me I can get whatever I want at Power's and put it on their tab," she confided to Imogene, but it went against her grain.

But at least she came first! At least she had Jack, if she did have to share him with Grammy. And Grammy made a fuss over her, in the beginning anyway. One night Grammy came out of the kitchen, bearing a cake she had beaten up and baked in secret and singing:

Happy birthday to you,
Happy birthday to you . . .

"What's going on?" said Jack before she could finish. "It ain't time for my birthday yet!"

Eventually she did learn to beat a dozen egg whites on a platter for an angel food cake, the way Grammy did, and she learned some of the largess of Aunt Em's kitchen—"Aunt Em said, *I hate a skimpy apple pie,*" she always quoted as she sliced in the extra apples and mounded the top crust, and in the same breath reminded me that Aunt Em had wanted my father to marry one of the Conard girls.

But she was unreconciled when I was born, in the last month and year of a decade that never ended for her. "If we'd waited until we could afford one, we'd never have had a baby," she said.

Still, they had waited several years. *I'd hate to think one of my daughters was doing something unnatural,* worried her mother, who suspected rightly that her daughters had a choice she never had. Sylva, living at Fort Peck while her husband worked among thousands of strangers on the new dam, had gotten a foolproof recipe from a woman she met there and sent it to my mother. Quinine and cocoa butter, mixed together in a saucer and left to harden, then broken into chunks. Its peculiar odor permeated my mother's top dresser drawer while its texture, rigid and melting at the same time, drew the fingers of curious little girls.

But a baby. Yes. If it was a boy, another Albert Hogeland.

Snow fell heavily that December, and the wind blew the roads shut. My father took her to Lewistown in plenty of time and left her with Aunt Rebie. She waited and chafed.

"Your dad was feeding cattle. He never got back to town to see me the whole ten days after you were born. The nurses thought my husband must be in the service."

A few days before Christmas he finally shoveled his way to town and brought her and the new daughter home to the log house. Grammy and Bill could hardly wait. A baby! A little girl. If they had been disappointed that she was not another Albert Hogeland, they forgot it when they saw her. And Uncle Theo was dying to see her. Were they going to name her after Grammy, he wanted to know?

"No!" said my mother. "Mary Rebecca."

"They had a big time over you. You were the first grand-child on both sides, and they all thought you were so smart— *Never saw so smart a kid,* Bill Hafer would say. Pretty soon you started saying it. I knocked that out of you."

She never thought she came first again.

ı ı ı ı ı ı ı

Life on the ranch stayed the same, but the thirties changed. The reforms of the Roosevelt administration brought a flow of cash into Montana and, eventually, a transformation of lives and landscape. The whole family had been jarred when my mother's oldest sister, Sylva, had married a boy from a starved-out homestead in the Judith Basin and gone with him to Fort Peck to work on the greatest of all New Deal work projects, the giant earth-filled dam that brought ten thousand jobs to the Montana highline and forever altered the Missouri River.

"Going to work for wages!" My father never could understand it. "How in the hell a man can go to work for some son of a bitch and punch his clock and take his orders, *when he's used to being his own boss—*"

Worse than not being your own boss was going on relief. A fourth of the population of Montana was getting public assistance during the worst of the depression, whether through the CCC, the WPA, or outright dole. Fifty years later my mother could name every one of their neighbors who had chosen shame over starvation.

"Ma was beside herself when Sylva got married and she found out his family had been on *relief*!"

Imperceptibly perhaps, the old rigorous life was coming to an end. The Rural Electrification Administration, delayed by World War II, came to our part of central Montana in 1946, when my mother had been married for ten years, and she threw out her kerosene lamps without nostalgia. Two years later Bell Telephone strung its wires as far as the ranch, and she could order her groceries by phone at the Olympian Grocery in Lewistown and have them waiting for her when she brought in the cream cans. When she was forty, we moved into a house with running water and a flush toilet. The Great Leveler had lifted its weight from Montana, easing my mother's life but at the same time impoverishing her.

You don't know what it is to do without! she accused her daughters. *I never had pretty clothes when I was in school! Never!*

Sylva's husband had made good at Fort Peck and gone from there to Grand Coulee Dam, and from Grand Coulee to the lofts in Bremerton where the ships were being designed to replenish the Pacific fleet. After the war, he and Sylva started their own construction business in booming, building-hungry Seattle. Imogene had her good job in Port Angeles. Nobody seemed strapped anymore. And with the war over, it was possible to buy cars again. Refrigerators. Even in Lewistown new stores full of frivolities were opening their doors. Some of the cousins' wives went to work in the new western-wear store and spent their salaries on cowboy boots and fancy fringed shirts and jeans for themselves and their children.

To be poor is to have less than others. In the thirties, as my father loved to point out, nobody had anything. My mother was not the only girl who went off to the Billings

normal school with cardboard in her shoes—far from it; she
went without, and her friends went without, and they laughed
and joked and let the wind whip snow around the eaves of
some isolated schoolhouse in the country while they charged
across the splintering softwood floor to the directions of a
square dance caller:

> *Lady round lady and the gent so low,*
> *Lady round lady and the gent don't go!*

She had as much as anyone, and more, because she had
met my father, and she felt loved for the first time in her life.

My mother finally told part of her story one afternoon on
a hillside north of Denton. My sister and I had brought a
picnic lunch and found the shade of a pine to spread it under.
We could see other pines in the distance, cropping through
the sandstones above the Judith River, and a speck of white
against the slope of the prairie: the two-room house where
my mother had come of age.

"We'd lost our homestead," she said. "Pa had to take
bankruptcy. But Ma had saved a little money from her teaching, and she managed to get this place by paying the taxes
on it."

I could remember the house when my grandmother Welch
still lived there. Tight white siding, a step up to the single
door in the end. Room enough for a bed and a dresser in the
one room, a coal range and a kitchen table in the other.
Drinking water dribbled through a tap in the bottom of a
Red Wing crockery cooler, never quite cool, never quite stale.
A ladder nailed against the wall led through a trapdoor to
the suffocating heat of the attic, where my aunt Imogene used
to sleep in the summertime. She could look out the tiny window and see bunchgrass blowing in the yard and tumble-
weeds ragging at the barbed-wire fence and the two tracks
of the road.

I had heard how my grandmother had gotten the place by paying the county its delinquent taxes, but the rest of the story my mother now told was new.

"The fellow that had owned this place, Tom Buler, wouldn't move off of it. He'd planted a crop, and the sheriff told Ma he had a right to stay and harvest it. So we holed up for the summer in an old line shack and waited for him to leave.

"Ma sent Pa over a time or two to talk to Buler, but it didn't do any good. He still wouldn't leave. So Ma waited until she saw Buler go to town, and then she loaded what she could in the wagon. She had Dave and me with her—I was fourteen. Pa must have been packing up another load at the shack. Buler showed up just as she was moving his furniture out in the yard and moving hers in."

My mother paused here. She realized, I think, for the first time the effect of her story on her audience. I and my sister and my sister's husband sat around her in the brittle grass, waiting to hear what happened next.

"Buler grabbed hold of Ma, like he was going to throw her out. Dave was— I guess Dave must have started back with the wagon to get another load.

"I picked up a chunk of stovewood, and I said, *You get your goddamned hands off my mother!*"

"What did Buler do then?" my sister asked.

"Do? He didn't do anything. He left."

After a moment of openmouthed silence, my brother-in-law began to laugh. He laughed so hard he had to lie on his back in the grass to get his breath. "One set of neighbors goes to town," he tried to explain, "and another set of neighbors comes galloping over the coulee with their furniture to move into their house—" He laughed until he was helpless; he could neither stop laughing nor explain the joke.

I watched the two tracks of the road blur between the stubble fields and disappear. The sun beat on the crust of topsoil bleached into powder under the sparse grass, and mirages trembled just out of reach. I wanted to laugh, but I felt dizzy; the thread of my mother's story dangled in the void. *You get your goddamned hands off my mother.*

I will never know her. I only hope I may be half as brave as she.

GOING TO
FORT PECK

Denton, Montana, 1919.

|||||||||||||||||||||||||||||||||||||||||||||||||

*O*n this late afternoon in April of 1934, two cars grind into sight through the wash of rain at twenty miles an hour, sometimes fifteen, sliding between the ditches and throwing up mud from their chains. The little black '28 Ford coupe and the black Model A, persistent as hornets as they round still another bend in the road, top another rise. Windshields are pocked with mud and streaked with rain, the side windows glazed with condensation and chill. But they roar on through gumbo and sparse gravel, skidding toward disaster and recovering while the rain sheets down.

The boy who drives the coupe is light-haired and slight and long past fatigue. His hands have cramped to the shape of the steering wheel from driving and fighting to stay on the road all the way from the Judith Basin. At first he talked to pass the time, but the man in the seat beside him has hardly answered since dawn. Ahead is more storm ceiling, and more rain that batters the skeleton sagebrush and the wavering muddy road.

The boy fights the front wheels of the coupe up the wobble of one more hill and squints through the streaks on the windshield at sod giving way to rolling gray current. The big river, the Missouri at last. He pulls over in the muddy stretch by the ferry and stops, unclenching his fingers.

The Model A chugs up beside him. Faces on the passenger side, Fexler's wife and the two children, float like pale blobs through the streaming windows.

He glances at his own passenger.

"Guess we got here," he ventures, but McVeigh says nothing.

A tap on his window. Fexler stands there, hunched in the rain, more rain dripping off the brim of his hat. "Guess we'll try to camp in them willows," he yells over the current.

As the gust of cold air invades the close atmosphere of the coupe the boy's eyes wander through the scudding gray rain toward the river, the stark black cottonwoods, and the ruts up from the ferry crossing on the other shore. His arms and shoulders feel slack with exhaustion, but he knows how long he can keep working after his muscles want to quit. If he tells his hands to lift themselves back on the wheel, he can drive down to the ferry. He has a two-bit piece. He sees himself paying it over to the ferryman. Driving out on the raft. Leaning back in his seat as the winch starts up, resting his arms, letting the rope tow him across the current. On the other side of the Missouri, that much farther from home, he can sleep in his car.

"You folks don't want to cross tonight and camp at the site?" he asks.

Fexler looks down at his shoes in the mud. "Like to do that," he says finally, "but we got to get some grub in them babies."

McVeigh stirs, shifts around on the seat. Rain drums on the coupe. Fexler busies himself with the toe of his shoe, scraping off mud on the running board.

"All right," the boy says, and both men look up. "Maybe we can get a fire going."

The early yellow shoots of willows grow a hundred yards downstream from the ferry. The boy drives through soggy grass and pulls over, scratching against willow twigs, to make room for the Model A.

"Would you look at it rain," says McVeigh. "Wonder if it's raining at home."

McVeigh just sits there, watching the rain come down, so the boy gets out and wades through last fall's grass and buck-brush until he is deep enough into the willow grove to be out of Mrs. Fexler's sight. Then he hunches over and un-buttons his fly. God, the relief! All of him seems to drain. From where he stands, on the trace of an old cattle trail, he can see a gravel bar and hear the current. He listens, straining for the sounds of construction or trucks on the other side, the clang of tools or the shouts of men. Tired as he is, he feels as if he could swim across. Get to the site! Get signed on, get to work.

Back in the clearing, Fexler is studying the rear bumper of his Model A as though for revelation.

"By golly," he says. "That tent musta worked itself loose. Thought I heard something hit on the Arrow Creek grade, but I couldn't see nothing."

"Dad?" calls the woman wearily. "The kids and I got to get out."

"Thought I had the sumbitch lashed on pretty good too."

In that moment the scene is imprinted in the boy's memory: the waning daylight, the willows beaded with rain. The man with his silly, repetitive justification of his lost tent. The exhausted woman and the two children in the other car, the morose McVeigh. They drag as heavily on him as his sodden woolen clothes. They remind him of his mother and father, whining, hanging on in their shack, and he shudders. If they could, they'd hang on to him to the grave. Is it because they are so old? Fexler and McVeigh both must be in their thirties, beaten down, teeth gone. All they hope for is a summer's work on the new dam, thirty dollars a week for the next few weeks, then home to the Judith Basin.

By God, he promises himself. *I'm never going to be afraid to let go and grab for my next chance.*

But they are men from home. He can't just walk off and leave them on this alien northern prairie, not if they need help.

"I got a piece of tarp we can maybe rig good enough to keep the rain off a fire," he offers, and Fexler looks almost happy.

| | | | | | |

In the morning's fine drizzle, after Mrs. Fexler has led the children in their coats and scarves into the brush and back again, after they have given up again on the fire and gone without coffee, straightening their clothes as best they can and combing their hair, they all climb back in the two cars and drive out of the willow grove to the ferry.

Fexler studies the clouds when he gets out to pay his two bits to the ferryman. "Believe it might clear off today."

The boy feels fine. His arms and shoulders ache from fighting the wheel through gumbo all day yesterday, but when has he not ached from work? He eases the coupe onto the sawed-board deck of the ferry and jumps out to block his wheels. For just a moment the roll of the current catches him off balance. Then he leans on the fender and watches the advance of the cottonwoods on the opposite bank as the winch tightens and the cable sways overhead. Seventy-five cents an hour is what they're paying truck drivers to haul dirt for the giant earth-filled dam at Fort Peck, and if he sleeps out under his tarp all summer and cooks for himself, he can save most of it.

| | | | | | |

"Three men up from Judith Basin County? Leonard Fexler? Delbert McVeigh? Ervin Noel? How old are you, Noel?"

"Twenty-one."

The foreman shakes his head. "You look like you're sixteen. By Christ. You sure you're big enough to reach the clutch on one of them trucks?"

Two years ago, when the road construction chief asked him if he knew how to drive a truck, he had answered, *Hell no, I never even saw one before,* and the chief laughed and told him to hang around for a while.

Now he says, "You're goddamn right. I can reach the clutch on anything you got around here."

The foreman shrugs. "They called your name in Judith Basin County. You're on."

He signs his name, pockets the truck keys, and turns from the head of the line, elated. Spread out before him is what he came for: a new landscape being carved out of the ancient line of gray hills between northern Montana and Canada, skinned of grass, a crawling panorama of trucks and dredgers and horse-drawn scrapers across the ocean of mud. It means flood control, it means a source of electrical power, it means ten thousand jobs. For him it means escape.

| | | | | | | |

He takes a deep breath of green lumber from the new barracks and thawing grass under his feet. He's at Fort Peck, he's signed on, and he'll work, by God, like he worked on the road crews and the going-broke trucking outfits from the Judith Basin to the North Dakota line, always keeping an eye out for what needed to be done, taking the time at the end of his shift to check oil and grease, to service his truck, working on his own time to make sure he'd always be the last man laid off. He knew when he registered for work on the dam that he'd be lucky to get on; they were taking the married men with families first, like Fexler and McVeigh. But by God, they called up three names from Judith Basin County, and he's one of the three, and here he is.

Fexler nudges him. "You plan to bunk in the barracks, Noel?"

"No, I figured I'd camp down by the river."

"Mind if we . . ."

| | | | | | | |

It rains. During the day it lets up to a drizzle, and gears howl as the Mack dump trucks roll up the grades with load after load of fill dirt for what the newspapers are calling one of the wonders of the world, the largest earth-filled dam ever built. All day the boy jolts in his truck, straining to reach the gears, muscling the wheels. After his shift, he's out greasing, servicing, before he leaves his truck on the line, always with his eye out for his main chance, making sure the foreman knows he's reliable. Indispensable. Finally at dusk, as the rain comes down harder, he's walking along the trail into the willows.

He could sleep in the barracks the government threw up last fall. But he has resolved from the first not to let room and board eat up his wages. And sooner or later it's bound to stop raining. Not in his whole life in dry Montana has he ever seen so much rain.

But waiting for him are the Fexlers, shivering in the rain, trying to fix something for the kids to eat over a fire under his tarp. The Fexlers knew when they came to Fort Peck that they wouldn't be able to get housing. Evidently the government didn't think about places for them to live when it was giving priority hiring to married men. But that's the government. A man has to look out for himself and his own. He'd like to wring Fexler's foolish neck for losing his tent. How could the man be so simple as not to check his load?

And McVeigh! His face gets longer every day.

"By God, McVeigh, you had the right idea leaving your old lady home with the kids where at least they can stay dry," Fexler tells him.

"Sure do wonder how she's getting along with all them chores to do by herself," is all McVeigh will say.

Then it rains some more. It makes what rain they've seen so far look like a sprinkle by comparison. It rains like somebody dumped all the water barrels in the world over Fort Peck. Rain sweeps down in sheets, washing mud off the damsite in gray and yellow waves, leveling out tracks, gouging new rivulets down from the hills in its pell-mell roar into the Missouri. The camp in the willows is ankle-deep in water. The tarp sags deeper and deeper with its load of water, finally sags off its willow poles and collapses.

And then it rains harder.

"We got to do something different than this!" the boy yells over the drum of rain on the roof of the coupe.

McVeigh shivers. He has wrapped his arms around himself, trying to warm his hands in his armpits, trying to shrink himself down to nothing. The boy knows how he feels. His clothes are clammy too. But damn McVeigh, anyway! He feels like kicking him right in his sorry hind end for letting his misery show, for sitting there all humped up in himself. He has to turn away to hide his revulsion.

A few yards away, through the swimming side windows, he catches a glimpse of a face in the Model A. He doesn't suppose the Fexler kids have had anything hot to eat since supper last night.

Rain runs through his saturated cap, into his hair, and down his shoulders as he pounds on the window until Fexler hears him and cranks it down a crack.

"The foreman and some of them were telling about a woman on the other side of the river"—the boy gestures to make himself understood—"who's running a boardinghouse."

Fexler shakes his head, mouthing something through the noise of the rain. He's got no more money for the ferry. No way to get back across the river.

"Neither do I! We'll go across on the construction bridge."

"Guards!" Fexler screams back. "They don't let private cars on that bridge!"

"Hell with the guards!"

The boy leads the way in the coupe. McVeigh just rides along, not asking any questions. The boy has to squint to see the approach to the bridge in the dusk and the rain, and how Fexler can see a damn thing through the mud he's throwing up behind him, he doesn't know. But as it turns out, they've got only one guard on the bridge this evening, and he's trying to keep out of the rain; he jerks his arms and yells something, but the boy guns the coupe past him and onto the bridge. Now if Fexler just has the guts to—he does. The Model A is following right behind him, across the slippery timbers, rattling over the roar of the Missouri.

The ranch buildings, when they find them, are just low sheds and a peaked house along the rain-blurred line between hills and darkening sky. Eyes loom up in the headlights— milk cows, standing dumb in the lee of one of the sheds.

Well yes, admits the woman who comes to the door, she's been renting out rooms to construction workers, but she's full up, has been for a month . . . She shakes her head. Probably ain't an empty room for rent between here and Glasgow. By golly, these construction workers, they been moving into Fort Peck like a buncha ants, and they're living in some of the awfullest places—you say you got kids waiting in the car?

She shakes her head again. "Only thing I got's a granary."

"The granary got a roof?"

She points to a shed in the corner of the pasture, a hundred yards away. Sure, get them kids in out of the rain. They can pay her when they get paid.

The boy unwires the granary door and holds up his lantern. Rain dins on the tin roof, and something scuttles out of sight of the light, but it's dry in here. If he can get a fire going in that barrel, it'll be warm.

Mouse dirt and wheat kernels crunch under his shoes as he goes to take a look. Mrs. Fexler, blinking in the light, leads in a child in each hand and bends over to unbutton wet coats.

"That woman let me borrow her broom," says Fexler. "I believe we'll have room to spread out if we can sweep up some of this crap."

In a few minutes, flames are leaping in the barrel and casting their red glow on the rafters and the shadowy junk in the corners. The boy rummages around and finds a piece of scrap iron he can set the coffeepot on. The fragrance of beans bubbles up. Mrs. Fexler is wringing out clothes and hanging them from nails to dry.

The boy winks at the little Fexler girl when he catches her watching him. Embarrassed, she hides her face against her mother.

"She's about the same age as my twin sisters," he explains.

"Hey," says Fexler suddenly, "where's McVeigh?"

"McVeigh!"

From the door of the granary, in the rays cast by the lantern across the sheeting rain, McVeigh is finally located right where they left him, a miserable hump in the passenger seat of the coupe.

"McVeigh, what in hell are you doing out there?"

McVeigh is crying. "I can't help it," he sobs. "I miss my wife so much. I want to go home."

| | | | | | | |

The boy stands in the door of the granary, savoring the luxury of dry clothes and a hot cup of coffee. It is Sunday morning, and it's still raining, although a pale light along the skyline to the east suggests it will not rain forever. On the other side of the river the trucks and dredgers are stilled, their crews sleeping off Saturday night in the barracks or in the tin-can-and-tarpaper hovels that have sprung up around the site. Behind him in the granary, the Fexlers are getting dressed. Everybody is glad that McVeigh headed home last night.

"Tain't gonna rain no more, no more," Fexler sings. "Now how in the *hell* can the old folks *tell* if it ain't gonna rain no more?"

The boy has been thinking. If he can find a sheltered cutbank somewhere, off a ways from the site, he can build himself a house. About eight by ten, he thinks, like one of those trailer houses some of the engineers pull behind cars. Celatex is what they're made of. He's priced it, and he figures he can get all the materials he needs, including a couple windows and linoleum for the floor, for about eighty-five dollars.

Bet you'll be glad to see your folks in the fall, Mrs. Fexler said to him last night after they all tried to calm down McVeigh.

There's nothing for me at home. No way to get ahead, he answered her, but it wasn't what he was thinking.

A dollar a day for driving a buck rake in haying season from first light until dark and a couple hours of chores after that. Sleeping in a bedroll, living on bad cooking. Worse than the fatigue is seeing the old men on the ranches around the basin—old geezers who have worked for wages since they were his age, never married because they couldn't afford it, stove up now from the years of jolting labor, snaggletoothed from the diet, still shuffling after enough money to buy tobacco and a place to sleep.

Then home in the fall with his sixty or seventy dollars, whatever he's managed to save, and his dad telling him to hand it over because the money a boy earns before he's twenty-one belongs by law to his father. Finally he and his next younger brother tell the old man to go to hell, they'll run away before they give over any more of the money they've worked for. But it's hard. Times are hard, and there are six younger children still at home. Nothing to eat. The homestead's failing, the family's on relief. Seems like his dad never has known how to take hold.

Heard you got a sweetheart! teased Mrs. Fexler last night.
Yeh. Her ma don't like me much, though.

Last year, finishing out the summer in his uncle's hayfield after the trucking outfit he'd hired on with went belly-up, he'd knocked off for lunch in the shade of the old cottonwood and seen the dark-eyed girl coming down from the house with his aunt. This here is Sylva Welch, his aunt told him, she'll be boarding with us. She's teaching the Pigeye school this winter. Sylva smiled, a little aloof. Close up, he could see she was older than him, close to thirty, though she was so small and slender. A serious-looking girl, a teacher, and then he thought, *Why the hell not? I'm going to be good enough for a teacher, by God.*

| | | | | | | |

This Sunday morning the boy leans in the doorway of the granary, finishing his coffee and watching the sky gradually clearing in the east. This Fort Peck project is a great thing, all right. Those old river bluffs will never be the same, and neither will he.

The little Fexler girl peeks out at him, and then hides when he grins at her. He thinks about kids of his own. And about seeing that his little sisters get to finish high school.

Working on Sunday afternoons and into the long summer twilights after his shift, he'll build his little Celatex house with a stove and a bed and a sound roof overhead. And an outhouse, by God, no more of this hunting up a wet sagebrush big enough to hide behind. In September he's going to marry Sylva.

| | | | | | |

"Ervin and I were married in Great Falls on a Saturday, September 29, 1934," Sylva wrote years later. "We bought our wedding things that morning and were married shortly after noon. His suit cost $17, my dress $10, and the wedding ring was $5."

Her mother grieved. Giving up a perfectly good teaching job to marry that boy? Giving up seventy-five dollars a month for him? Going up to Fort Peck to live on the site with all that riffraff? Sylva, her hope, her studious bright girl, her delicate one.

But Sylva had no misgivings. She had seen him that noon in the hayfield, a slight boy with blue eyes and a grin, light-haired, sunburned to where he'd rolled his shirtsleeves. She went to a few country dances with him during that fall and into the winter, whenever he was back in the Judith Basin between trucking jobs. When he went to Fort Peck, she wrote to him.

And then she married him and moved into the little house he had built under the cutbank near the Missouri River. She knew her mother was worried to death that she would get pregnant right away.

Ervin had battened the house on the outside with tarpaper and banked it against the coming winter, so airtight that the lamp went out if more than two people sat inside and breathed up the oxygen. Her steamer trunk was too big to get inside the house, so he built a little platform just outside the door for it and covered it with a tarp. On top of the trunk sat the washtub. And behind the house, in the cutbank, he dug a cave for potatoes and set a box of sawdust to hold milk.

Sylva said afterward that the worst part was the boredom, having nothing to do during the long hours while he was working. She made curtains for the tiny house and cooked on top of the ovenless coal stove. She went for long walks over the prairie, through the sagebrush and the shortgrass, following the little trails through the coulees, watching the aspens turn color.

It was an empty country, depleted of game, drained of life. Those primeval hills had folded back from the river, unchanged for thousands of years while hunter-gatherer cultures came and went, while the plains tribes lived out their brief horse culture and died of disease and white depredations, while the white settlers, the sodbusters and honyockers and scissorbills, lived out their briefer cycle and fled the drought of the 1920s. She saw a soddie or two, empty and caving in, last traces of another generation's dreams. Beyond that she saw the colorless grass, the bleached sky of a prairie fall. She could almost believe in endlessness.

| | | | | | |

But all during the summer of 1934, shanty settlements have been springing up around the construction site with names like Wheeler, Delano, Park Grove, New Deal, Square Deal, and Cactus Flats. Sylva finds herself living on the edge of Park Grove, near New Deal. She substitute-teaches one day in a school swollen to sixty mismatched pupils. The rest of the time she learns how to live in a boomer settlement. The water from the Park Grove well looks cloudy, so she buys water in a barrel from a man who hauls it in a truck. No electricity, no plumbing. Every tarpaper shack has another little structure out in back. Hundreds of rows of shacks, hundreds of rows of outhouses. No wonder the water is cloudy.

Nobody in 1934 sees the outhouses, of course. They will be invisible until, half a century later, Sylva's snapshots expose their comic multiplicity to a generation that has hidden from itself the necessity for basic, practical means of emptying bladder and bowels.

But back and forth on the hundreds of little paths of 1934, pretending not to see each other, trot the wives and children of construction workers. These shanty towns—and outhouses—are homes for the thousands of dependents of men who registered in their home counties for work on the dam. They are thankful to get off relief. They have no future. Behind them are the parched homesteads, the starvation, the hopelessness of hundreds of families like the Noels. What they do have is now, and now is a weekly paycheck.

Then Ervin comes home from his shift, aching from the hours of jousting with heavy equipment. He brings in the washtub and sets it in front of the stove, fills it with hot water and soaks his muscles back to life. Then he is ready to go again. He and Sylva are young, and they have enough money for beer. Fort Peck on a Saturday night!

First thing, they want to see a beer parlor. They've grown up with Prohibition, they know all about the bootleggers and the rumrunners whose road across Montana from Canada cut off just below the homestead where Sylva grew up. She remembers the lone headlights at night, and sometimes the sound of a car running without headlights. But a beer parlor! To walk in and sit down at a table with other young men and women and order a beer, big as life! Riffraff, her mother might snort, but they seem like nice people to Sylva. She and Ervin drink a few and dance a lot and move on to the next joint. Fort Peck has plenty of beer parlors and honky-tonks.

And if this isn't living close enough to the brink for a bookish girl from north of Denton, she can enjoy the dizzy knowledge of the red-light districts flourishing behind the boomer settlements. What is a red-light district like? What on earth does a real prostitute look like? Nothing is easier than to find out. Full of beer, giggling, she and Ervin and a crowd of their friends pile into two or three cars and drive through the rutted streets of Wheeler to peer out at the women waiting in the doorways. The couple in the car with Ervin and Sylva have brought along their four-year-old son, who struggles to see whatever his parents are so interested in. When Ervin pulls over and stops, the little boy sees his chance and dives out of the car.

"Jerry! Come back!" screams his mother.

Bewildered, the child hesitates in the street. The woman in the opposite doorway stares back. Then she steps back into her house and slams her door. Other doors slam up and down the street. Lights are blown out in windows. All is silent.

Then laughter gusts up in the car.

"What did you think she was going to do to Jerry?" they tease his mother.

Sylva laughs until she cries. She has never had such a good time, and she has Ervin close beside her as they drive slowly home in the small hours. She senses the durability in Ervin as she gets to know him better, and she never regrets the chance she took when she resigned her safe teaching job and married him.

| | | | | | |

Then winter set in, blizzard by blizzard. In January and February of 1936 a record-breaking cold spell settled over Montana. Thermometers went down to forty degrees below zero and stayed there for a month. The government thermometer showed sixty-two below.

"The air was still with a frosty haze hanging in the sky," Sylva wrote. "Cottonwood trees snapped and crackled during the night. We could not drive our car because the grease got so thick it cracked the ring gear in the rear end. So Ervin bundled up and walked over to take the train to the work site."

The Mack dump trucks had no heaters and no doors. The drivers put cardboard in front of the radiators and around the lower part of the cabs to try to keep some heat on their legs. They muffled their faces and pulled on extra gloves, but the cold seeped down until their fingers and their feet went numb. *I'll drive one more round and pack it in,* Ervin would promise himself, and drive one more round and another until he finished his shift. At the end he was so stiff he could scarcely walk.

What can Sylva do, besides have his hot supper ready? Watch him grimace as, lowering himself into the washtub of hot water, he feels the heat stab through his extremities? Herself be the first out of bed every morning, her breath white in the frigid space, her bare feet wincing on the linoleum, brittle with the pervasive cold, to crumple the newspaper and touch the match in the coal stove? Luckily they have plenty of wood and coal, hauled by Ervin before the weather set in, and she can keep their tiny room warm during the daytime.

But every night after midnight, she feels Ervin sigh and stretch in the bed beside her, then heave out as gently as he can to keep the blankets over her. She hears him moving around the small space, getting dressed, bundling into coat and cap and gloves. Then a brief freezing draft before he quickly closes the door behind him.

Left to herself, Sylva rolls over into the warm hollow on his side of the bed and drowses her way back to sleep. She knows where he is going in the forty-below night, and she knows when he will come back to catch another couple of hours' sleep before he has to get up for his shift. Over at the site, the graveyard shift is in full swing. The welding shop is lit up and sizzling with sparks, and in the welding shop Ervin has found a foreman who will take the time—in the small private hours, when his crew is well occupied—to teach Ervin the trade.

How else does a young man learn to weld? How would he even know what welding was, when he grew up on a homestead outside Utica, Montana, where the only metal-working he ever saw was what the local blacksmith could hammer over a forge? He might have learned Latin at the Utica high school, but not metalworking, if he could have gone to high school instead of going to work. No, he had to wait until he got to Fort Peck, where he was quick to notice the advantages the skilled workmen held over the unskilled, like himself. And then he had to happen upon the older man generous enough with his own time and skill to hold open the door for him.

Welding is done in a shop, where it's warm—that's one reason he wants to learn. For another, the certified welders make twice what the truck drivers do. Still another reason—he sees it dimly, his eyes full of the revolution of sparks from the blast of his torch against the steel as he bends to his solder—is that the welder always looks ahead. He can count on today's job, today's wages, and tomorrow's wages as well; and therefore the young man goes without sleep night after night to light his torch in the welding shop and practice the skill he needs for his escape.

He doesn't know it yet, but in the spring of 1936 the call will go out for welders at the Fort Peck construction site. He will be ready. He'll take the government tests for welder certification and pass all but one.

He's got the right to repeat the test once, but there's a hitch: the welding superintendent has to give his permission, and he won't. Half a century later, Sylva and Ervin still speculate why, why, why, when he'd worked so hard for it, when he had the right. Was it pressure from the older skilled work-men, old drinking buddies from years of jobs, who feared the young aspirants for higher-paying trades? Was it bad-mouthing from the superintendent's friend Morris, a good old boy whom Ervin somehow had gotten crosswise with? They'll never know.

There's always next year, says the welding superintendent. *Just don't push it. Hell, what's a year to a young fellow like you?*

No, by God. I got the right to retake it now.

Can't nobody tell you a goddamn thing? N-O, no. And another thing—you're laid off as of now. Maybe three days off the job will cool you down.

| | | | | | |

None of this Ervin knows yet as he bends over his solder, getting it perfect. He likes this new, close work with his hands, the precision, the control. He squints through his visor into the cascade of sparks, aiming at the core. If he knew the future, would he still take the chance?

| | | | | | |

One way to look at it, Sylva, we got three days and a weekend. Let's go to Grand Coulee, they got a call out for welders . . .

So Sylva and Ervin will throw a few things in the car and drive to Grand Coulee, Washington, where another dam is under construction, another boom under way, another flood of the eager, the hungry, the foolish and wise. Ervin will retake his test on Friday and go to work at Grand Coulee on Monday for $1.50 an hour. Twice the pay of truck drivers! They won't look back except to retrieve the rest of their possessions from the tiny house at Fort Peck. What if the Grand Coulee job only lasts from June to cold weather? They'll have savings by then, and they'll drift through eastern

Washington ahead of the winter on what Ervin can earn doing metal repair. A welder can live anywhere.

What do you think, Sylva? How'd you like to spend a winter in San Francisco?

Oh! San Francisco!

What'll we do with our lives, Sylva?

Oh—I'd like a little house, painted white, with two bedrooms.

Tell you what I'd like to learn next, Sylva, and that's drafting.

| | | | | | |

A roar of the acetylene torch, a final cascade of sparks, and the welder straightens from his solder.

THE UNWANTED CHILD

Left to right: Sylva, A. P. Welch (holding Doris), Kathryn, Imogene, 1914.

| | | | | | | | | | | | | | | | | | | | | | | | | | | | | | | | | | | | | | | | | | |

$\mathcal{D}$ecember 1958. I lie on my back on an examination table in a Missoula clinic while the middle-aged doctor whose name I found in the Yellow Pages inserts his speculum and takes a look. He turns to the sink and washes his hands.

"Yes, you're pregnant," he says. "Congratulations, Mommy."

His confirmation settles over me like a fog that won't lift. Myself I can manage for, but for myself and *it*?

After I get dressed, he says, "I'll want to see you again in a month, Mommy."

If he calls me Mommy again, I will break his glasses and grind them in his face, grind them until he has no face. I will kick him right in his obscene fat paunch. I will bury my foot in his disgusting flesh.

I walk through the glass doors and between the shoveled banks of snow to the parking lot where my young husband waits in the car.

"You're not, are you?" he says.

"Yes."

"Yes, you're not?"

"Yes, I am! Jeez!"

His feelings are hurt. But he persists: "I just don't think you are. I just don't see how you could be."

He has a theory on the correct use of condoms, a theory considerably more flexible than the one outlined by the doctor I visited just before our marriage three months ago, and which he has been arguing with increasing anxiety ever since I missed my second period. I stare out the car window at the back of the clinic while he expounds on his theory for the zillionth time. What difference does it make now? Why can't he shut up? If I have to listen to him much longer, I will kill him, too.

At last, even his arguments wear thin against the irrefutable fact. As he turns the key in the ignition his eyes are deep with fear.

"But I'll stand by you," he promises.

I I I I I I I

Why get married at eighteen?

When you get married, you can move into married student housing. It's a shambles, it's a complex of converted World War II barracks known as the Strips, it's so sorry the wind blows through the cracks around the windows and it lacks hot-water heaters and electric stoves, but at least it's not the dormitory, which is otherwise the required residence of all women at the University of Montana. Although no such regulations apply to male students, single women must be signed in and ready for bed check by ten o'clock on weeknights and one on weekends. No alcohol, no phones in rooms. Women must not be reported on campus in slacks or shorts (unless they can prove they are on their way to a physical education class), and on Sundays they may not appear except in heels, hose, and hat. A curious side effect of marriage, however, is that the responsibility for one's virtue is automatically transferred from the dean of women to one's husband. Miss Maurine Clow never does bed checks or beer checks in the Strips.

When you get married, you can quit making out in the back seat of a parked car and go to bed in a bed. All young women in 1958 like sex. Maybe their mothers had headaches or hang-ups, but *they* are normal, healthy women with normal, healthy desires, and they know the joy they will find in their husbands' arms will—well, be better than making out, which, though none of us will admit it, is getting to be boring. We spend hours shivering with our clothes off in cars parked in Pattee Canyon in subzero weather, groping and being groped and feeling embarrassed when other cars crunch by in the snow, full of onlookers with craning necks, and worrying about the classes we're not attending because making out takes so much time. We are normal, healthy women with normal, healthy desires if we have to die to prove it. Nobody has ever said out loud that she would like to go to bed and *get it over with* and get on with something else.

There's another reason for getting married at eighteen, but it's more complicated.

| | | | | | |

By getting married I have eluded Dean Maurine Clow only to fall into the hands of in-laws.

"We have to tell the folks," my husband insists. "They'll want to know."

His letter elicits the predictable long-distance phone call from them. I make him answer it. While he talks to them I rattle dishes in the kitchen, knowing exactly how they look, his momma and his daddy in their suffocating Helena living room hung with mounted elk antlers and religious calendars, their heads together over the phone, their faces wreathed in big grins at his news.

"They want to talk to you," he says finally. Then, "Come on!"

I take the phone with fear and hatred. "Hello?"

"Well!!!" My mother-in-law's voice carols over the miles. "I guess this is finally the end of college for you!"

I I I I I I I

A week after Christmas I lean against the sink in my mother's kitchen at the ranch and watch her wash clothes.

She uses a Maytag washing machine with a wringer and a monotonous, daylong chugging motor which, she often says, is a damn sight better than a washboard. She starts by filling the tub with boiling water and soap flakes. Then she agitates her whites for twenty minutes, fishes them out with her big fork, and feeds them sheet by sheet into the wringer. After she rinses them by hand, she reverses the wringer and feeds them back through, creased and steaming hot, and carries them out to the clothesline to freeze dry. By this time the water in the tub has cooled off enough for the coloreds. She'll keep running through her loads until she's down to the blue jeans and the water is thick and greasy. My mother has spent twenty-five years of Mondays on the washing.

I know I have to tell her I'm pregnant.

She's talking about college, she's quoting my grandmother, who believes that every woman should be self-sufficient. Even though I'm married now, even though I had finished only one year at the University of Montana before I got married, my grandmother has agreed to go on lending me what I need for tuition and books. Unlike my in-laws, who have not hesitated to tell me I should go to work as a typist or a waitress to support my husband through college (after all, he will be supporting me for the rest of my life), my grandmother believes I should get my own credentials.

My mother and grandmother talk about a teaching certificate as if it were a gold ring which, if I could just grab it, would entitle the two of them to draw a long breath of relief. Normally I hate to listen to their talk. They don't even know you can't get a two-year teaching certificate now, you have to go the full four years.

But beyond the certificate question, college has become something that I never expected and cannot explain: not something to grab and have done with but a door opening, a glimpse of an endless passage and professors who occasionally beckon from far ahead—like lovely, elderly Marguerite Ephron, who lately has been leading four or five of us through the *Aeneid*. Latin class has been my sanctuary for the past few months; Latin has been my solace from conflict that otherwise has left me as steamed and agitated as my mother's whites, now churning away in the Maytag; Latin in part because it is taught by Mrs. Ephron, always serene, endlessly patient, mercilessly thorough, who teaches at the university while Mr. Ephron works at home, in a basement full of typewriters with special keyboards, on the translations of obscure clay tablets.

So I've been accepting my grandmother's money under false pretenses. I'm not going to spend my life teaching around Fergus County the way she did, the way my mother would have if she hadn't married my father. I've married my husband under false pretenses, too; he's a good fly-fishing Helena boy who has no idea in the world of becoming a Mr. Ephron. But, subversive as a foundling in a fairy tale, I have tried to explain none of my new aspirations to my mother or grandmother or, least of all, my husband and his parents, who are mightily distressed as it is by my borrowing money for my own education.

"—and it's all got to be paid back, you'll be starting your lives in *debt*!"

"—the important thing is to get *him* through, *he's* the one who's got to go out and face the world!"

"—what on earth do you think you'll do with your education?"

And now all the argument is pointless, the question of teaching certificate over quest for identity, the importance of my husband's future over mine, the relentless struggle with the in-laws over what is most mine, my self. I'm done for, knocked out of the running by the application of a faulty condom theory.

"Mom," I blurt, "I'm pregnant."

She gasps. And before she can let out that breath, a frame of memory freezes with her in it, poised over her rinse tub, looking at me through the rising steam and the grinding wringer. Right now I'm much too miserable to wonder what she sees when she looks at me: her oldest daughter, her book-ish child, the daydreamer, the one she usually can't stand, the one who takes everything too seriously, who will never learn to take no for an answer. Thin and strong and blue-jeaned, bespectacled and crop-haired, this girl could pass for fifteen right now and won't be able to buy beer in grocery stores for years without showing her driver's license. This girl who is too miserable to look her mother in the face, who otherwise might see in her mother's eyes the years of blight and disappointment. She does hear what her mother says:

"Oh, Mary, no!"

| | | | | | | |

My mother was an unwanted child. The fourth daughter of a homesteading family racked by drought and debt, she was only a year old when the sister nearest her in age died of a cancerous tumor. She was only two years old when the fifth and last child, the cherished boy, was born. She was never studious like her older sisters nor, of course, was she a boy, and she was never able to find her own ground to stand on until she married.

Growing up, I heard her version often, for my mother was given to a kind of continuous oral interpretation of herself and her situation. Standing over the sink or stove, hoeing the garden, running her sewing machine with the permanent angry line deepening between her eyes, she talked. Unlike the stories our grandmothers told, which, like fairy tales, narrated the events of the past but avoided psychological speculation ("Great-great-aunt Somebody-or-other was home alone making soap when the Indians came, so she waited until they got close enough, and then she threw a ladle of lye on them . . ."), my mother's dwelt on the motives behind the darkest family impulses.

"Ma never should have had me. It was her own fault. She never should have had me if she didn't want me."

"But then you wouldn't have been born!" I interrupted, horrified at the thought of not being.

"Wouldn't have mattered to me," she said. "I'd never have known the difference."

What I cannot remember today is whom my mother was telling her story to. Our grandmothers told their stories to my little sisters and me, to entertain us, but my mother's bitter words flowed past us like a river current past small, ignored onlookers who eavesdropped from its shores. I remember her words, compulsive, repetitious, spilling out over her work—for she was always working—and I was awed by her courage. What could be less comprehensible than not wanting to be? More fearsome than annihilation?

Nor can I remember enough about the circumstances of my mother's life during the late 1940s and the early 1950s to know why she was so angry, why she was so compelled to deconstruct her childhood. Her lot was not easy. She had married into a close-knit family that kept to itself. She had her husband's mother on her hands all her life, and on top of the normal isolation and hard work of a ranch wife of those years, she had to provide home schooling for her children.

And my father's health was precarious, and the ranch was failing. The reality of that closed life along the river bottom became more and more attenuated by the outward reality of banks and interest rates and the shifting course of agribusiness. She was touchy with money worries. She saw the circumstances of her sisters' lives grow easier as her own grew harder. Perhaps these were reasons enough for rage.

I recall my mother in her middle thirties through the telescoped eye of the child which distorts the intentions of parents and enlarges them to giants. Of course she was larger than life. Unlike my father, with his spectrum of ailments, she was never sick. She was never hospitalized in her life for any reason but childbirth, never came down with anything worse than a cold. She lugged the armloads of wood and buckets of water and slops and ashes that came with cooking and washing and ironing in a kitchen with a wood range and no plumbing; she provided the endless starchy meals of roast meat and potatoes and gravy; she kept salads on her table and fresh or home-canned vegetables at a time when iceberg lettuce was a town affectation.

She was clear-skinned, with large gray eyes that often seemed fixed on some point far beyond our familiar slopes and cutbanks. And even allowing for the child's telescoped eye, she was a tall woman who thought of herself as oversized. She was the tallest of her sisters. "*As big as Doris* is what they used to say about me!"

Bigness to her was a curse. "You big ox!" she would fling at me over some altercation with my little sister. True to the imperative that is handed down through the generations, I in turn bought my clothes two sizes too large for years.

All adult ranch women were fat. I remember hardly a woman out of her teens in those years who was not fat. The few exceptions were the women who had, virtually, become a third sex by taking on men's work in the fields and corrals;

they might stay as skinny and tough in their Levi's as hired hands.

But women who remained women baked cakes and cream pies and breads and sweet rolls with the eggs from their own chickens and the milk and butter and cream from the cows they milked, and they ate heavily from appetite and from fatigue and from the monotony of their isolation. They wore starched cotton print dresses and starched aprons and walked ponderously beside their whiplash husbands. My mother, unless she was going to be riding or helping in the hayfields, always wore those shapeless, starched dresses she sewed herself, always cut from the same pattern, always layered over with an apron.

What was she so angry about? Why was her forehead kneaded permanently into a frown? It was a revelation for me one afternoon when she answered a knock at the screen door, and she smiled, and her voice lifted to greet an old friend of hers and my father's from their single days. Color rose in her face, and she looked pretty as she told him where he could find my father. Was that how outsiders always saw her?

Other ranch women seemed cheerful enough on the rare occasions when they came in out of the gumbo. Spying on them as they sat on benches in the shade outside the horticulture house at the county fair or visited in the cabs of trucks at rodeos, I wondered if these women, too, were angry when they were alone with only their children to observe them. What secrets lay behind those vast placid, smiling faces, and what stories could their children tell?

My mother believed that her mother had loved her brother best and her older sisters next best. "He was always The Boy and they were The Girls, and Ma was proud of how well they did in school," she explained again and again to the walls, the stove, the floor she was mopping, "and I was just Doris. I was average."

Knowing how my grandmother had misjudged my mother, I felt guilty about how much I longed for her visits. I loved my grandmother and her fresh supply of stories about the children who went to the schools she taught, the games they played, and the books they read. School for me was an emblem of the world outside our creek-bottom meadows and fenced mountain slopes. At eight, I was still being taught at home; our gumbo road was impassable for most of the school months, and my father preferred that we be kept safe from contact with "them damn town kids," as he called them. Subversively I begged my grandmother to repeat her stories again and again, and I tried to imagine what it must be like to see other children every day and to have a real desk and real lessons. Other than my little sister, my playmates were mostly cats. But my grandmother brought with her the breath of elsewhere.

My mother's resentment whitened in intensity during the weeks before a visit from my grandmother, smoldered during the visit itself, and flared up again as soon as my grandmother was safely down the road to her next school. "I wonder if she ever realizes she wouldn't even have any grandchildren if I hadn't got married and had some kids! *The Girls* never had any kids! Some people should never have kids! Some people should never get married!"

With a child's logic, I thought she was talking about me. I thought I was responsible for her anger. I was preoccupied for a long time with a story I had read about a fisherman who was granted three wishes; he had used his wishes badly, but I was sure I could do better, given the chance. I thought a lot about how I would use three wishes, how I would use their potential for lifting me out of the present.

"What would you wish for, if you had three wishes?" I prodded my mother.

She turned her faraway gray eyes on me, as though she

had not been ranting about The Girls the moment before. "I'd wish you'd be good," she said.

That was what she always said, no matter how often I asked her. With everything under the sun to wish for, that unfailing answer was a perplexity and a worry.

I was my grandmother's namesake, and I was a bookworm like my mother's older sisters. Nobody could pry my nose out of a book to do my chores, even though I was marked to be the outdoor-working child, even though I was supposed to be my father's boy.

Other signs that I was not a boy arose to trouble us both and account, I thought, for my mother's one wish.

"Mary's getting a butt on her just like a girl," she remarked one night as I climbed out of the tub. Alarmed, I craned my neck to see what had changed about my eight-year-old buttocks.

"Next thing, you'll be mooning in the mirror and wanting to pluck your eyebrows like the rest of 'em," she said.

"I will not," I said doubtfully.

I could find no way through the contradiction. On the one hand, I was a boy (except that I also was a bookworm), and my chores were always in the barns and corrals, never the kitchen. *You don't know how to cook on a wood stove?* my mother-in-law was to cry in disbelief. *And you grew up on a ranch?*

To act like a boy was approved; to cry or show fear was to invite ridicule. *Sissy! Big bellercalf!* On the other hand, I was scolded for hanging around the men, the way ranch boys did. I was not a boy (my buttocks, my vanity). What was I?

"Your dad's boy," my mother answered comfortingly when I asked her. She named a woman I knew. "Just like Hazel. Her dad can't get along without her."

Hazel was a tough, shy woman who rode fences and pulled calves and took no interest in the country dances or the "running around" her sisters did on weekends. Hazel never used lipstick or permed her hair; she wore it cut almost like a man's. Seen at the occasional rodeo or bull sale in her decently pressed pearl-button shirt and new Levi's, she stuck close to her dad. Like me, Hazel apparently was not permitted to hang around the men.

What Hazel did not seem interested in was any kind of fun, and a great resolve arose in me that, whatever I was, I was going to have . . . whatever it was. I would get married, even if I wasn't supposed to.

| | | | | | |

But my mother had another, darker reason to be angry with me, and I knew it. The reason had broken over me suddenly the summer I was seven and had been playing, on warm afternoons, in a rain barrel full of water. Splashing around, elbows and knees knocking against the side of the barrel, I enjoyed the rare sensation of being wet all over. My little sister, four, came and stood on tiptoe to watch. It occurred to me to boost her into the barrel with me.

My mother burst out of the kitchen door and snatched her back.

"What are you trying to do, kill her?" she shouted.

I stared back at her, wet, dumbfounded.

Her eyes blazed over me, her brows knotted at their worst. "And after you'd drowned her, I suppose you'd have slunk off to hide somewhere until it was all over!"

It had never crossed my mind to kill my sister, or that my mother might think I wanted to. (Although I had, once, drowned a setting of baby chicks in a rain barrel.) But that afternoon, dripping in my underpants, goose-bumped and ashamed, I watched her carry my sister into the house and then I did go off to hide until it was, somehow, all over, for she never mentioned it at dinner.

The chicks had been balls of yellow fuzz, and I had been three. I wanted them to swim. I can just remember catching a chick and holding it in the water until it stopped squirming and then laying it down to catch a fresh one. I didn't stop until I had drowned the whole dozen and laid them out in a sodden yellow row.

What the mind refuses to allow to surface is characterized by a suspicious absence. Of detail, of associations. Memories skirt the edge of nothing. There is for me about this incident that suspicious absence. What is being withheld?

Had I, for instance, given my mother cause to believe I might harm my sister? Children have done such harm, and worse. What can be submerged deeper, denied more vehemently, than the murderous impulse? At four, my sister was a tender, trusting little girl with my mother's wide gray eyes and brows. A younger sister of an older sister. A good girl. Mommy's girl.

What do I really know about my mother's feelings toward her own dead sister? Kathryn's dolls had been put away; my mother was never allowed to touch them.

"I'll never, never love one of my kids more than another!" she screamed at my father in one of her afternoons of white rage. The context is missing.

| | | | | | | |

During the good years, when cattle prices were high enough to pay the year's bills and a little extra, my mother bought wallpaper out of a catalog and stuck it to her lumpy walls. She enameled her kitchen white, and she sewed narrow strips of cloth she called "drapes" to hang at the sides of her windows. She bought a stiff tight cylinder of linoleum at Sears, Roebuck in town and hauled it home in the back of the pickup and unrolled it in a shiny flowered oblong in the middle of her splintery front room floor.

Occasionally I would find her sitting in her front room on her "davenport," which she had saved for and bought used, her lap full of sewing and her forehead relaxed out of its knot. For a moment there was her room around her as she wanted it to look: the clutter subdued, the new linoleum mopped and quivering under the chair legs that held down its corners, the tension of the opposing floral patterns of wallpaper, drapes, and slipcovers held in brief, illusory harmony by the force of her vision.

How hard she tried for her daughters! Over the slow thirty miles of gumbo and gravel we drove to town every summer for dentist appointments at a time when pulling teeth was still a more common remedy than filling them, when our own father and his mother wore false teeth before they were forty.

During the good years, we drove the thirty miles for piano lessons. An upright Kimball was purchased and hauled home in the back of the pickup. Its carved oak leaves and ivories dominated the front room, where she found time to "sit with us" every day as we practiced. With a pencil she pointed out the notes she had learned to read during her five scant quarters in normal school, and made us read them aloud. "F sharp!" she would scream over the throb of the Maytag in the kitchen as one of us pounded away.

She carped about bookworms, but she located the dim old Carnegie library in town and got library cards for us even though, as country kids, we weren't strictly entitled to them. After that, trips home from town with sacks of groceries included armloads of library books. Against certain strictures, she could be counted on. When, in my teens, I came home with my account of the new book the librarian kept in her desk drawer and refused to check out to me, my mother straightened her back as I knew she would. "She thinks she can tell one of my kids what she can read and what she can't read?"

On our next visit to the library, she marched up the stone steps and into the mote-filled sanctum with me.

The white-haired librarian glanced up inquiringly.

"You got *From Here to Eternity?*"

The librarian looked at me, then at my mother. Without a word she reached into her drawer and took out a heavy volume. She stamped it and handed it to my mother, who handed it to me.

How did she determine that books and dentistry and piano lessons were necessities for her daughters, and what battles did she fight for them as slipping cattle prices put even a gallon of white enamel paint or a sheet of new linoleum beyond her reach?

Disaster followed disaster on the ranch. An entire season's hay crop lost to a combination of ancient machinery that would not hold together and heavy rains that would not let up. A whole year's calf crop lost because the cows had been pastured in timber that had been logged, and when they ate the pine needles from the downed tops, they spontaneously aborted. As my father grew less and less able to face the reality of the downward spiral, what could she hope to hold together with her pathetic floral drapes and floral slipcovers?

| | | | | | |

Bundled in coats and overshoes in the premature February dark, our white breaths as one, my mother and I huddle in the shadow of the chicken house. By moonlight we watch the white-tailed deer that have slipped down out of the timber to feed from the haystack a scant fifty yards away. Cautiously I raise my father's rifle to my shoulder. I'm not all that good a marksman, I hate the inevitable explosive crack, but I brace myself on the corner of the chicken house and sight carefully and remember to squeeze. Ka-crack!

Eight taupe shapes shoot up their heads and spring for cover. A single mound remains in the snow near the haystack. By the time my mother and I have climbed through the fence and trudged up to the haystack, all movement from the doe is reflexive. "Nice and fat," says my mother.

Working together with our butcher knives, we lop off her scent glands and slit her and gut her and save the heart and liver in a bucket for breakfast. Then, each taking a leg, we drag her down the field, under the fence, around the chicken house, and into the kitchen, where we will skin her out and butcher her.

We are two mid-twentieth-century women putting meat on the table for the next few weeks. Neither of us has ever had a hunting license, and if we did, hunting season is long closed, but we're serene about what we're doing. "Eating our hay, aren't they?" says my mother. "We're entitled to a little venison. The main thing is not to tell anybody what we're doing."

| | | | | | | |

And the pregnant eighteen-year-old? What about her?

In June of 1959 she sits up in the hospital bed, holding in her arms a small warm scrap whose temples are deeply dented from the forceps. She cannot remember birthing him, only the long hours alone before the anesthetic took over. She feels little this morning, only a dull worry about the money, money, money for college in the fall.

The in-laws are a steady, insistent, increasingly frantic chorus of disapproval over her plans. *But, Mary! Tiny babies have to be kept warm!* her mother-in-law keeps repeating, pathetically, ever since she was told about Mary's plans for fall quarter.

But, Mary! How can you expect to go to college and take good care of a husband and a baby?

Finally, *We're going to put our foot down!*

She knows that somehow she has got to extricate herself from these sappy folks. About the baby, she feels only a mild curiosity. Life where there was none before. The rise and fall of his tiny chest. She has him on her hands now. She must take care of him.

Why not an abortion?

Because the thought never crossed her mind. Another suspicious absence, another void for memory to skirt. What she knew about abortion was passed around the midnight parties in the girls' dormitory: *You drink one part turpentine with two parts sugar. Or was it the other way around? . . . two parts turpentine to one part sugar. You drink gin in a hot bath . . .*

She has always hated the smell of gin. It reminds her of the pine needles her father's cattle ate, and how their calves were born shallow-breathed and shriveled, and how they died. She knows a young married woman who begged her husband to hit her in the stomach and abort their fourth child.

Once, in her eighth month, the doctor had shot her a look across his table. "If you don't want this baby," he said, "I know plenty of people who do."

"I want it," she lied.

No, but really. What is to become of this eighteen-year-old and her baby?

Well, she's read all the sentimental literature they shove on the high school girls. She knows how the plot is supposed to turn out.

Basically, she has two choices.

One, she can invest all her hopes for her own future in this sleeping scrap. *Son, it was always my dream to climb to the stars. Now the tears of joy spring at the sight of you with your college diploma . . .*

Even at eighteen, this lilylicking is enough to make her sick.

Or two, she can abandon the baby and the husband and become really successful and really evil. This is the more attractive version of the plot, but she doesn't really believe in it. Nobody she knows has tried it. It seems as out of reach from ordinary daylight Montana as Joan Crawford or the Duchess of Windsor or the moon. As she lies propped up in bed with the sleeping scrap in her arms, looking out over the dusty downtown rooftops settling into noon in the waning Eisenhower years, she knows very well that Joan Crawford will never play the story of her life.

What, then? What choice is left to her?

What outcome could possibly be worth all this uproar? Her husband is on the verge of tears these days; he's only twenty himself, and he had no idea what trouble he was marrying into, his parents pleading and arguing and threatening, even his brothers and their wives chiming in with their opinions, even the minister getting into it, even the neighbors; and meanwhile his wife's grandmother firing off red-hot letters from her side, meanwhile his wife's mother refusing to budge an inch—united, those two women are as formidable as a pair of rhinoceroses, though of course he has no idea in the world what it took to unite them.

All this widening emotional vortex over whether or not one Montana girl will finish college. What kind of genius would she have to be to justify it all? Will it be enough that, thirty years later, she will have read approximately 16,250 freshman English essays out of an estimated lifetime total of 32,000?

Will it be enough, over the years, that she remembers the frozen frame of her mother's face over the rinse tub that day after Christmas in 1958 and wonders whether she can do as much for her son as was done for her? Or that she often wonders whether she really lied when she said, *I want it?*

Will it be enough? What else is there?

JANUARY 1922

Mary Welch about 1935.

||||||||||||||||||||||||||||||||||||||||||||||||

$\mathcal{T}$ he world is reduced to a north slope, oppressed by the weight of snow in the sky and the dull prairie, where for months the snow has blown and drifted over last summer's ruts that follow a barbed-wire fence east and out of sight. Along the distant north rim, hiding the Judith River breaks, a few miniaturized black pines crop up between the gray sky and the gray snow of late afternoon. But on this side of the slope there is no sign of river current, no movement. It will be dark in an hour and already it is twenty degrees below zero.

At first the loaded wagon is only a dark speck as it crawls into focus from the west. As it looms larger, shapes can be discerned: the man on the spring seat holding the stiff lines in mittened hands, the dark-haired woman beside him, and, shivering and blanket-wrapped in the back of the wagon with the few crates of household goods, the three children.

| | | | | | | |

Another time and place. My mother remembers running in the dusk to keep up, crying, stumbling in the rutted snow, panting and sobbing and begging her father to let her back into the wagon. Later she understood that he had been making her and her brother and sister run behind the wagon to keep them from freezing.

| | | | | | |

Now, as though a black-and-white photograph gradually clears and sharpens, features emerge from the distance. His face, once handsome, is beginning to shrink over the skull, his nose and chin drawing together and releasing his eyes into a jerky life of their own. Her face, too, is drawn with twelve years of privation and silent grief, framed unbecomingly with hair she has twisted under to hide the gray, but her eyes are set on the road she has yet to travel. For another mile or two it will skirt the prairie before it leaves the relative shelter of the river breaks with their black etchings of jack pine and plunges across empty white space toward an isolated man-made structure.

Perched against a knob of bare rock where it can be seen for miles is an unpainted frame shack, perhaps ten years old and already weathered to gray and warped, but more durable than anyone in the wagon can know: it will stand here on this dome for at least another sixty-five years. It is the Baldy Dome (pronounced Ballydome) school, and its teacher has resigned in the middle of the school year and moved back to town.

The horses' breaths hang under their bowed heads in white puffs that fade over their hooves. They are crossbred draft mares, shaggy as bears in their overgrown manes, their little eyes peering out of their blinders. The man slaps the lines over their backs, and they plod through the wire gate, around to the lee side of the school, and stop.

The children jump from the back of the wagon, stamping their feet on the crusted snow to get back their feeling. The little boy and girl spar at each other, silent and implacable, but the twelve-year-old girl, Imogene, tries the door of the teacherage and waits on the step for her mother to come and unlock it. From that sheltered step, where the snow has drifted in a fine hard powder, Imogene glances back at the schoolyard, curious for a first glimpse of the place where she will live and go to school for the next six months: the coal shed; the empty, unrevealing windows of the school; the girls' and boys' outhouses at their regulation 150 feet apart—the whole enclosed from the prairie by a barbed-wire fence.

Working quickly to keep warm, the man and woman carry her few boxes into the teacherage. He still has the three-hour drive home with the team and wagon and chores to do when he gets there. She must unpack and bed down the children and prepare the next morning's lessons, the first lessons she will have taught in nearly twenty years. Meanwhile the teacherage is locked in an icy stillness that seems worse for being within walls, the claustrophobic iciness of the tomb that permeates wool coats and mufflers and blunts the senses and paralyzes hands and feet on its way to the bone.

She lights the kerosene lamp and sets it on the table. Shadows leap out, and the shape of the unfamiliar rubbish left behind by the young man who resigned, and the children's faces. She turns, sees that her husband has carried in kindling and coal and is striking a match on the iron range. Almost at once the rapid heat layers the windows with frost, and for the first time they see that a pane is missing.

She waits, watching her husband to see what he will do. For months she has been watching him, hardly aware of when she began or why she secretly tallies the signs that he still has initiative. And now she sees how, with his numbed hands, he hammers the end out of one of the boxes and, stopgap, tacks it over the gaping hole in the window.

Relieved, she heats a skillet and begins to cook a meal. Home-cured salt pork, home-canned beans and tomatoes, a loaf of the bread she baked this morning to see them through this first week. With the good smells of familiar food rises the illusion that nothing has changed, and in silence they all gather around the table, pick up hastily unpacked forks and knives in fingers still awkward from cold, and commence to eat with no sense that for them as a family this is a first meal and a last. After tonight they will never again be the same. Although separately they will all carry its scars through their subsequent time and travail, that fifteen-mile, three-hour wagon journey from the homestead to the Ballydome never can be retracted.

But for tonight, blessedly, they cannot read the future; here, around this table in the circle of lamplight, they are unaware of their moment of grace. They eat with the hunger of people who have been very cold. Only the two youngest, Doris and David, carry on their unforgiving warfare with the ferocity of children who know that their place in the world is threatened. In ten minutes they have finished supper. He departs quietly for his drive home alone in the dark; she turns to heat water on the stove for dishes. Later, by lamplight, she will study.

| | | | | | |

"Ma went out to teach when I was eight," said my mother, who in that other time and place had been Doris, the insignificant, "and nothing was the same after that. It must have been terrible for Pa, batching all by himself during the week on the homestead. She'd come home on the weekends, and try to clean and wash clothes and cook and bake enough for the next week. It never was the same. I never had another birthday cake after Ma went out to teach."

"She made the most wonderful birthday cakes," said Imogene. "Four layers. Whoever's birthday it was got to choose the colors of the layers. Any combination of white, pink, yellow, chocolate. She only had two cake pans, so she would bake two layers and then two more layers. Once—it would have been Kathryn's last birthday, her third—Ma baked her cake and set it up on a shelf, but Kathryn scooted a chair over and got her fingers into the frosting and ate a big hole in the side of the cake. When Ma caught her, she just spread the frosting over the hole as best she could. I didn't understand why Kathryn didn't get a hiding. I knew I would have."

| | | | | | | |

A.P. and Mary Elizabeth Welch had been among the thousands of young people who streamed into Montana during the homestead rush of 1910 to 1914. Knowing that theirs was a last chance at living the frontier dream, at following the westering tradition that had drawn their grandparents out of their safe seaboard villages and their parents to settle the Midwest, believing in the assurances of fertile land and prosperity, of eighteen inches of annual rainfall and four dollars a bushel for wheat, armed with their youth and health and ignorance, A.P. and Mary were among the first young couples to detrain at Lewistown, Montana, in 1910, buy a team and a plow and a spring wagon, and drive off into the void to stake their claim to 320 dryland acres.

In 1910 the prairie was empty. The Indians had been driven out, and a few cowhands kept track of cattle over the thousands of acres in central Montana that the old Huffine outfit claimed as grazing range. It would be over two years before neighbors would take up claims on the slope along the Judith River breaks that A.P. and Mary had chosen. But they were undeterred. They had a plan. A.P. would travel among the far-flung settlers of central Montana by team and wagon, selling insurance to tide them over until they could harvest a crop, while Mary stayed on the claim and did the chores and proved up. Nothing was insurmountable for them. They were young and they were invulnerable.

A photograph of A.P. taken just before they left Iowa for Montana shows him in dress clothes against a formal studio backdrop. Smiling in immaculate white linen and dark serge, he is good-looking, unsuspecting. Though he has nothing to hide, all is hidden; his eyes look directly out of the photograph at the granddaughter who searches his face for a trace of the old man she barely remembers.

One of a large family of Canadians, son of a second marriage, with several much older stepbrothers who would inherit whatever his father might have scraped together, A.P. had come down to Iowa and started a hardware store and met and married Mary. Now, at the time of the photograph, he is about to launch out on the biggest, most romantic venture of his life, as fabulous as the legends of his loyalist ancestors who fled New York for Ontario in the wreckage of the Revolution, or of his grandfather and great-uncles who struck out from eastern Canada with nothing but their rifles, axheads, and some salt. Though A.P. is town-bred, though his own work experience has been in the sociable, loquacious mercantiles in the small towns of central Canada and the American Midwest, he does not doubt that he can homestead. He knows nothing about prairie distance or silence. In the photograph he holds his little daughter, Sylva, by the hand, obviously proud of the tiny dark-eyed girl in her light piqué coat and matching bonnet.

And so, in 1910, A.P. and Mary, with little Sylva, filed on the north slope of the prairie twenty miles north of what, in three more years, would be the town of Denton. They built a shack and a shed from lumber hauled from Lewistown. In August Imogene was born.

That country north of Denton can seem desolate today,

especially when snow settles in and glimpses of farm lights are lost behind the swells of land and the horizon vanishes. In 1910 it really was desolate. A.P., out selling his insurance, had the best of it at first. A surviving letter of Mary's still sounds of romance, or perhaps of bravado. *You must come and visit us next summer,* she wrote to her youngest sister, *on our Montana ranch.*

But the sister, whom she had helped to raise, for whom little Sylva was named, died that year two thousand miles away. Mary went eighteen months without seeing another woman, and the experience caused her to hallucinate.

"The spring was a quarter of a mile from the shack," said Imogene. "In the summer of 1911 she used to wait until the cool part of the day to walk down with her buckets for her water. And she began to see shapes on the other side of the spring, the shapes of women, beckoning to her. A few years later she told an aunt that they looked like the shapes of her dead mother and her dead sister. She decided she was losing her mind. She had Sylva and me depending on her, Pa gone for days, no one else for miles. So she began to go for her water at noon, in the full sun. She never saw the shapes again."

| | | | | | |

That fall, Mary went out to milk the cow and feed the stock, leaving three-year-old Sylva in the shack to watch the baby. A chinook wind had swept down out of the west, tearing up grass and weeds and clods of dirt at forty or fifty miles an hour. As Mary led the horses out of the shed and around to the water trough, the wind caught the high corner of the shed, which she and A.P. had built without realizing the prevailing direction of the winds. It lifted the shed off its sandstone footings and flung it down on its side, a hundred feet away, leaving the cow tethered and startled in thin gritty air and Sylva screaming in terror from the window where she had been watching.

A.P., off in Lewistown on his insurance business, said he felt something tell him to get home as fast as he could. He harnessed a borrowed team and started at a dead run. By the time he reached the homestead, the wind had died down, the shed was a pile of splintered boards, and Sylva was in hysterics. Until Mary appeared, leading the horses around the wreckage of the shed, Sylva had supposed she was crushed to death.

"Sylva's been afraid of wind all her life," said Imogene.

The borrowed team was nearly crippled with exhaustion. "A.P.'s idea of driving is to run 'em up the hill and let 'em jump off," was how Mary's father summed up the story. All of the Iowa family made fun of A.P.'s ineptitude on the land.

After the shock of the first year, it was Mary, the farm-bred oldest daughter of that rural Iowa autocrat, who best withstood the rigors of homesteading. Neighbors moved out along the river breaks, hammering up shacks on their 320s, and that was better for Mary. She taught Sylva how to walk the quarter of a mile to the nearest of the new neighbors in case of trouble. She broke sod for a garden and kept her cow fresh and fed the extra milk to the pigs, fed her flock of chickens and canned her produce and put down pork in brine. No one in her care ever was hungry, or unclothed. She made over her sisters' cast-off clothes for her little girls and sewed the scraps into ugly, utilitarian quilts. Her shack was clean and warm, if unlovely. What she could do, she did.

But almost from the first she seems to have blamed A.P. for the betrayal that was Montana. Certainly he was not her father or one of her brothers, and his land was not the flat fertile acreage of Iowa. He had not been raised to the land, and he must have realized before Mary did that he hated farming. He liked people, he loved his sociable insurance circuit, he knew everybody for miles. Apple Pie Welch, they called him. But plowing alone on the north slope, trying to hold together the implements he did not know how to repair, his eyes began to jerk.

| | | | | | |

"Denton is situated in the heart of one of the richest agricultural regions of the west. Within the short space of four months a new town has sprouted and many enterprises have sprung into existence. . . . There is every evidence that Denton will be a city of some magnitude. It is situated on the new line of the Chicago, Milwaukee, and St. Paul railroad and is mid-way between Great Falls and Lewistown," bragged the new Denton newspaper in September of 1913. "Every business man in Denton is a live wire."

By 1920 the newspaper had changed its tune, if not its bravado: "The man who weakens on the Judith Basin without being absolutely compelled to do so, is going to regret his lack of faith."

| | | | | | |

It was not A.P.'s fault when the promised eighteen inches of annual rainfall dwindled during the drought years of 1919, 1920, and 1921 to less than six inches a season, when wheat shriveled from twenty-five bushels the acre to less than three, when the mistreated, desiccated, eroded land rose in dust clouds, when the boom-bust cycle of the homestead economy drove thousands of couples like him and Mary into foreclosure and bankruptcy, sent the banks spiraling into disaster, and blighted the hopeful, boastful little communities like Denton.

In his *Montana: High, Wide, and Handsome* (1943), Joseph Kinsey Howard detailed the lies and the tragic good intentions behind the Enlarged Homestead Act of 1909, from James J. Hill's vision of a farm family on every 320 acres of Montana's millions of acres of public domain, to the national clamor for increased wheat production to choke the growing "German threat," to the crazy theories of dryland farming, the deep plowing and repeated cultivation that were supposed to conserve moisture but in fact speeded up soil erosion in the dry years and reduced hundreds of thousands of acres of virgin grassland to dust. Worse were banks that represented eastern and midwestern finance companies or individual capitalists: "Certainly it was bad banking. It couldn't survive four successive years of drouth followed by one of history's worst winters (1920–21), or mismanagement and ignorance, or ruthless government-enforced deflation. So Montana lost 38 per cent of its state banks and 30 per cent of its national banks, a fifth of its farms, half of its manufacturing establishments, nearly half of its retail businesses, 15 per cent of its population, and some of its towns."

Bad banking, bad farming, bad luck. We still look for ways to externalize the dream gone sour, to use cause and effect to distance ourselves from human misery.

What was happening to A.P. and Mary was worse than drought; they were racked and ruined by cause and effect closer to the bone even than Howard's outrage at the Federal Reserve System and without Howard's solace in fixing the blame "outside." Kathryn, their third little girl, born in 1912, had an abnormality of her right eye. A.P. and Mary borrowed money to get her to a good doctor, who diagnosed a cancerous brain tumor. He removed the eye, a postponement. Nothing else to do, he told them, but wait until the end.

A snapshot of the family taken by a visiting sister of Mary's during the summer of 1915 catches them, oddly, shelling peas. Mary has carried two kitchen chairs out into the yard, in the full sun. She sits in one chair with the dishpan in her lap and pea pods in her hands, as intent on her easy, boring task as though it claims her full concentration, as though she is unaware of the picture being taken or even that it has been posed. Her face and body already are set in familiar taut lines, carved deeper by the unrelenting light and shadows of the sun. Her hair is beginning to gray around her face. She will not look up, and yet her contained rage makes it hard to look away from her. Her visiting father, slumped in the other chair, is deflated in his shirtsleeves and full white mustache as he shells his peas. Sylva also shells peas dutifully.

But the other children. Imogene, five, squats in the foreground, her hair tangled and her face vacant. She is pretending she is an animal perhaps, imagining her way out of this bleached yard of uncut buffalo grass and the smell of pea pods and the hot knot of anger in the pose. Kathryn sits apart, on an overturned bucket. Her hands are clenched in her lap; she wears her eye patch. What can be seen of her square little face and her three-year-old body in her shapeless pinafore is as contained and inward-looking as her mother's, line for line.

In the intense moment, Doris is easily overlooked. But she is there. Dressed in a long smock whitened by the fierce Montana sun, she has crawled into the brittle grass behind the pea shellers and sat up, examining something she has found with a baby's total absorption.

Mary knows she is pregnant again. Years later she will remark that she felt sorry for Doris that summer. She fed her and changed her, but had no love left for her.

Only A.P. is missing.

l l l l l l l

Between 1921 and 1925, one out of every two Montana farmers lost his place by mortgage foreclosure. When, in spite of the pleas and exhortations of the Denton *Recorder,* the first of the neighbors along the Judith River breaks gave up and packed what they had left to pack, A.P. and Mary joined with others to give them a farewell party. Soon there were too many departures, too few to see them off. It was an end of times, a death of expectations. Of all those dreamers who had poured into Montana between 1910 and 1914, merchants and musicians and doctors and tailors and teachers and bank tellers and clerks in search of free land and opportunity and romance, sixty thousand had left Montana and their abused, parched homesites by 1925. *The land seemed to be mourning for them,* remembered a daughter of failed homesteaders, *and for everyone.*

But not A.P., not Mary. They had nothing. In the whole of central Montana, in the fabulous Judith Basin, apex of the Golden Triangle of wheat, no one had money to pay for insurance. Many could not even buy seed wheat. But Mary did not know what it was to give up, and she would not let A.P. falter. Her scars seemed only to deepen her resolve. She would find a way, not only to save their land but to pay back her father for the debts incurred for little Kathryn.

Twenty years earlier, as a girl in Iowa, Mary had taught school. She had had to battle for the opportunity. Her father had opposed her attending high school, pointing out that not only was her education costing money, it was losing her the wages she might have earned while she was studying. Mary defied him; she moved to town and scrubbed floors to pay for her board while she finished high school, went on to normal school, and finally got a school of her own. But when she married and came to Montana with A.P., she let her teaching certificate lapse. Married women did not teach.

But a hundred dollars a month! Children still had to go to school, even in hard times. Every dried-out little community still had its one-room school.

Mary began a correspondence course and studied at night to renew her certificate. *"Amo, amas, amat,"* she recited to her uncomprehending family. By May of 1922 she was ready to take the Montana State Teachers Examination, to be held at the county courthouse in Lewistown. Unlucky Doris, the date of the examination fell on her birthday. There would be no more baking of four-layered cakes.

| | | | | | |

Mary had hoped, in the fall of 1922, to get the teaching position at their own school, a quarter of a mile from their homestead. But the local school board was split; neighbors were jealous. Getting a school to teach was a prize in those hard years. The hundred-dollars-a-month salary could be the difference between eating and going hungry. For Mary to earn it gave the Welches an unfair edge. The board hired an outsider.

But rumor went around the county in November that the Ballydome school was going to be vacant, that the young male teacher had resigned and would be leaving after Christmas. Dr. Cunningham in Denton got wind of it and sent word out to the homestead by Sylva that Mrs. Welch should apply. They all were being very closemouthed. But Mary laid her plans, even though the Ballydome meant the three-hour drive back and forth by team and wagon, even though it meant splitting up the family. Sylva, in high school by now, would continue to board in Denton with Dr. Cunningham. A.P. would have to get along on his own. The three younger children, Imogene and Doris and David, would go with Mary. They were a strong point in favor of her being hired. Because they would add substantially to the Ballydome's enrollment and therefore would increase the district's share of state funding, they might offset the disadvantage of her being a married woman.

"We were told to keep quiet about it," said Imogene. "On the very last day before our school dismissed for Christmas, I was to tell the teacher that Doris and David and I wouldn't be back. But I was to wait until the last minute. Ma must have been terrified that word would get around and she would somehow lose the Ballydome job."

| | | | | | |

Dr. Cunningham was one of several women whose fragmentary stories converge on Mary's during those crucial years. A teacher until she began to lose her hearing, she had gone to Idaho and studied dentistry as an expedient. Sometime after 1913 she had come to Denton with her pliers and her treadle-powered drills and set up a circuit practice that took her all over the Judith Basin.

Doris waited one dim afternoon by the window overlooking the alley, listening to the slap of the treadle and the slow whine of the drill as Dr. Cunningham bore down on her mother's molars. When the whine died, Doris glanced around. Dr. Cunningham was beckoning to her. Reluctantly Doris left the window and approached the chair where her mother half reclined with her face drained and her fingers locked on the leather supports.

Dr. Cunningham motioned to the speckled tin basin; she wanted Doris to hold it while she drilled. So Doris took the basin and stood by the chair while Dr. Cunningham pumped away at her treadle with one foot to start up her drill again. As it ground into the tooth Mary gave a strangled start, and Dr. Cunningham stepped back. Doris held the basin for her mother's mouthful of bloody spittle and grit. Then Dr. Cunningham advanced again; the slow foot-powered drilling would take hours.

"How old was Dr. Cunningham when you boarded with her?" I once asked Sylva.

"Very old," said Sylva, now eighty herself. Then she smiled at the irony of her answer. "I was only fourteen. She would have seemed old to me. Her hair was white, and she wore it in a braid around her head. By then she was completely deaf, and she used an ear trumpet for people to shout through."

Sylva sat by her Seattle window, trying to remember more for me. Her own hair was white by now, and thin. In that diffuse coastal light, kinder than the hard Montana sunlight of her girlhood, she seemed as fragile as the memories she tried to recover of a woman big and strong enough to be a dentist in the early years of the century, a woman silent and isolated in her deafness.

"Sometimes she talked to me, even though I was so young. I have the feeling now that she was lonely. One thing I remember her telling me was that she had left her husband, years ago. And she had had a little boy. When the little boy died, her husband came to the funeral drunk. She told me, *I never could forgive him that.*"

| | | | | | |

Another unrecorded shadow who hints at the nuances, links, thrills, and textures of Mary's life was Laurel Watters, the neighbor's wife who, until drought and debts drove her family out of the basin, used to pile her small children with Mary's in the back of the spring wagon and gallop hell-for-leather with her over the sagebrush and gullies to the post office at Coffee Creek for the mail. The empty prairie held few obstacles, and Mary's mares loved to run. Imogene, huddled in the deep shelter of the wagon box with other small shrieking bodies, survived several of those glorious spine-cracking stampedes through snapping sage and the surprised flight of birds and the scent of alkali rising on their dust. "How we must have looked, us kids hanging on, Ma and Mrs. Watters on the wagon seat, probably one or both of them pregnant. It was their idea of a good time."

In that explosive moment, prairie vanishing under the strides of the mares, wind in the women's faces and the song of meadowlarks dissolving after them, in that hot moment of blue sky and pounding escape, it is not hard to imagine the good time for women who had been brought up never to admit to fun or pleasure.

| | | | | | |

Even more shadowy was the German woman who lay in one of those blistered shacks as the drought bore down, too sick to tend her eight children or even to stand on her feet. Being a Kuhn and sick in Montana in 1919 must have held its own terrors; two years earlier, wartime hysteria had swept over the state, darkening its politics and awakening paranoia in those who, like the editor of the Helena *Independent,* wondered, "Are the Germans about to bomb the capital of Montana? Have they spies in the mountain fastnesses equipped with wireless stations and aeroplanes? Do our enemies fly around our high mountains where formerly only the shadow of the eagle swept?" In Lewistown the citizens had dragged the German textbooks out of the county high school and burned them in the street; roused by the externalized threat, they may also have set fire to the high school itself. Arson was suspected but never proved when it burned to the ground.

North of Denton, however, no one had tormented the Kuhns, although Imogene stood in a circle with her schoolmates to stare at the towheaded little German-speaking children when they showed up with their smelly lunch buckets on the first day. And the next spring Mary hitched her mares to the wagon one morning and, leaving Sylva to care for her two little ones and taking nine-year-old Imogene along to help carry water, drove to the Kuhns' shack where the woman had lain for days.

She built a fire in the range and boiled tubs of water lugged up from the creek and set the accumulated mounds of soiled clothes to soak in the yard while she swept out the shack and started a baking of bread and a crock of beans large enough to last several days. Out in the unfenced yard again, up to her elbows in the steaming suds, she scrubbed every shirt, sheet, and pair of trousers for the family of ten on her board and dropped them into the boiling rinse tub where she stirred them with a broomstick, lifted them out, and wrung them in her red hands. Then, with the washtubs emptied into the pale drought-stricken grass behind the shack and turned upside down to drain in the lean-to, with all those clean wet shirts and sheets and trousers flapping in the undeflected light, she went back into the stark heat of the shack and took the dozen loaves out of the oven and heated the flatirons on the back of the stove. As the clothes quickly dried in the sunlight she carried them in, sprinkled them, and ironed them. Then she heated fresh water on the stove and gave Mrs. Kuhn a bath.

"Is there anything else I can do for you?" she asked, when she had finished.

"Take my baby," said the sick woman.

Little Ruby was seven months old.

"I'll take her," said Mary, "until you're well enough to fetch her."

| | | | | | |

After the winter at the Ballydome, Mary Elizabeth Welch taught in country schools for another thirty-five years. Schools that no longer exist—Danvers, Duck Creek, Shiny Mountain, Straw. A year here, a year there. Unwilling to give tenure, the local school boards rarely kept a teacher longer. But if a child in a district was having trouble learning to read, that school board often would try to get Mrs. Welch for a year. She had assembled a life raft of self-taught reading methods, and she saved many flounderers.

She managed the money for her daughters to go away to normal school long enough to get their own teaching certificates. (She would have managed for David, too, but he ran away.) Sylva taught at the Pigeye, Imogene at the Ballydome and Duck Creek and Roy, and Doris at the Conard school—where she met the young cowboy named Jack Hogeland.

Sometimes during those years, A.P. stayed with Mary in whichever dim one-room teacherage she was occupying at the time. Other times he stayed alone at the homestead. He was used to being alone. I have only the slightest memories of him—the feel of his hand in mine, brown eyes lingering on me, his toothless mouth.

But when I was very small, my parents ranched on the lower Judith, just under the bluffs from the old Welch homestead. A.P. occasionally would hike down through the bluffs to play with me, and I retain a sense of delight in those interludes. And yet, in the middle of a game, some notion would overtake him. One minute we would be chasing each other through the wild grass, the next minute I would turn around to see his brown-suited little figure trotting back up the bluffs through the sagebrush. And I remember the hard edges of the shadows and the smell of alkali and the way he never would turn or even slow down when I screamed, "Goppy! Come back!"

Mary, on the other hand, returns to me from some deeper source than memory. Her gestures, the quick movements of her hands, are imprinted on mine. She is there when I knead bread or comfort a child or pick up a pen. Sometimes I imagine her square figure turning from the teacherage stove where she has been poking up the coal fire, and I see her face with the arched brows and the compressed mouth and the permanent lines of sadness, and for a moment it is I who turn from the stove, my face seared with the indelible lines of hers.

She taught me to read. And sometimes I stayed with her, attending her school for a few sporadic weeks, living with her in the teacherage on bread and bologna from Longin's store and milk from the postmistress's cow. But I was not staying with her at Straw that night she walked a mile to the grain elevators and woke up the manager and used his telephone to call my mother and father for help.

Only Mary had seen the deterioration in A.P. that led finally to the scene I never witnessed but feel as though I had: the exclamation breaking the night-bound silence of the teacherage, the brief scuffle at the door. Then his gray head, his nightshirt gleaming white in the moonlight as he crawls through the three strands of barbed wire and dances across the neighboring wheat field. *You can't catch me, Mary!*

| | | | | | | |

To get to the cemetery today, drive down the wide main street of Denton with its two or three pickups parked at the curb by the café and the gas station and the post office. Spaced widely between these few living businesses are the empty lots, the traces of foundations, and the weathering boarded-up relics of the innocent days.

"There's sure nothing left in Denton," remarks my mother. "There's where the hotel was. There's where the old Seiden Drug was."

We turn right off the highway, onto the narrow gravel road that winds up through desiccated grass and dust and the buzz of grasshoppers to the cemetery ridge.

Here, on the crest of the ridge in full exposure to the sun and the winter storms, lie the few acres of graves. How many graves for a town the size of Denton is always my first thought, and how unsheltered is my second. Below in the town are the ample green tops of the cottonwoods and succor from the sun, but there is no water for irrigation up here on the ridge, and no trees. Paths are raked, and the native grass is kept mowed to three-inch sharp stubble. The graves of A.P.

and Mary Elizabeth Welch lie side by side, with little Kathryn's between them; they share one gravestone.

After a few minutes of silence, my mother and I wander apart among the graves, reading the inscriptions. Although the oldest graves go back only about seventy-five years, many are marked with wooden headboards by families who could not afford stones, and their names and dates have weathered to illegibility.

Many, picked out by borders of small smooth stones, are the tiny graves of children. And many of the markers that can be read are dated 1918, the year of the great flu epidemic. Some list the names of several children from the same family who died within the space of a few weeks or years. Wandering here among the forgotten, I find myself wondering how many women's lives came unhinged here at a time when to be crazed was commonplace.

I remember a story Imogene told, of Mary standing at Kathryn's grave for a long time, and how she finally raised her head and said, "I'd give everything I have if I could only have her back."

And then she would have turned, leading little Ruby (whose mother after a year or two did get well enough to come and fetch her), and walked back down that road to whatever labor lay ahead of her.

And I remember how we drove through ground blizzards and thirty-below-zero weather from Lewistown to Denton one winter, and how the cars behind us in the funeral procession crept up this road with their headlights dim through the furious snow; how the Methodist minister stood bareheaded only a moment over Mary's casket, while most of us huddled in the warmth of our cars; and how the greenhouse flowers turned black almost on impact with the icy air as they were lifted out of the hearse.

| | | | | | |

Amo, amas, amat. In the story of how Mary scraped and labored and shouldered on, and of the awful price she paid, this remains. She survived, and she handed on the tools for survival to those she could reach.

But at some time and place she and A.P., locked in their grief, diverged beyond reach. There is no accounting, finally, for Mary's continued endurance; no way of accounting for the will that sustained her on a road where A.P. could not follow, to the Ballydome in January of 1922. Some sources of strength, apparently, are irrevocable.

ALL BUT
THE WALTZ

Mary Hogeland and A. P. Welch, 1942.

|||||||||||||||||||||||||||||||||||||||||||||||||

During the long summer of 1982 I could forget for weeks at a time what was wrong with my husband. Those mornings dawned, one after another, in the transparent blue that foretold hundred-degree heat by noon, and he slept while I woke slowly in the pattern of light cast through the birch leaves outside our window, and he slept while I showered and pulled on a cotton dress and sandals for the office. I was expecting a baby in September, and my every exertion, heaving myself out of a chair, carrying the breakfast plates to the sink, letting myself out the back door and down the steps to my car in the already sweltering morning, cost me a deeper investment in my cocoon of self-absorption.

I had never supposed I would be pregnant again, not after twenty years. As my body swelled and my pace slowed in a sensation of suspended time, I remembered the pregnant teenager I had been as I might have remembered another woman, a passing acquaintance turned up again after more than twenty years. I drove to work already panting for breath in what passed for morning cool, along the residential streets of Havre where sprinklers plied the lawns for their allotted hours in the drought, and at five o'clock, arching my back against the ache, I drove home through the haze of dust that had filtered in from the fields. My feet and hands had swollen from the heat until I could not wear my shoes or wedding ring. I felt as though I would always be pregnant.

Except for occasional shortness of breath, Bob was still himself. Earlier in the spring he had driven out to the farm every day at first light for the brief frenetic weeks of spring seeding, but now, in the midsummer space between seeding and harvest, he had little to do but worry about the drought. He got up at noon, had breakfast downtown, drank coffee, and talked about rain with the other farmers.

By the beginning of the 1980s, Havre no longer rocked all night long as it had in the glory days of oil and gas exploration on the highline. The big poker games downtown had closed when the mudmen and the landmen and the drillers and toolpushers and roughnecks went broke or moved to Wyoming in search of new oil developments or, like Bob, went into soberer lines of work. But there were little poker games around town, at the Oxford Bar or PJ's Lounge, for a man looking for a distraction from the weather. At two or three in the morning I would hear the familiar sound of his Wagoneer in the driveway and rouse as Bob slipped into bed beside me, his arm raised to encompass mine as I turned, heavy-bellied, into the curve of his back. He had not yet, not perceptibly, begun to lose muscle tone.

In January he had had the flu, and it seemed to hang on. Sometimes, heading down the three back steps toward his Wagoneer, he had to stop and double over, gasping to get his breath in great racking heaves that left him exhausted. There seemed to be no reason for his lack of breath; he had no other symptoms.

"You ought to see a doctor," I said.

"Oh hell, I'm all right."

As the winter wore on he admitted that the boys down at

the coffee shop were urging him to get in and see the doc. Hell, maybe it was mono.

I made an appointment with the doctor for him, but he didn't show up for it.

I had plenty else to think about. Bob and I had been married four years, had been together seven years, and my pregnancy seemed too good to be true. I was undergoing amniocentesis and furnishing a nursery and dreaming about this baby as I had not had the time or inclination when, in my teens, my other children had been born.

Besides, it didn't seem possible that Bob could be sick. He was too crazy, too lucky, too full of the zest of living.

The son of a Kansas cattleman, Bob had left the ranch early for the glamour of the oil patch. Starting out as a roughneck, he went on to sell tools and oil field supplies, then to operate a fleet of water trucks, then to his own drilling rigs. He rode the roller coaster of oil and gas exploration and production, addicted like a gambler to the upward swoops and the adrenaline rushes, landing on his feet when he hit bottom, starting over on another of his nine lives. He came to Havre in the early 1970s, broke, to make a new start drilling gas wells into the shallow Judith River and Eagle formations. He went broke again and lost his rigs, but then he hit a lucky streak, scalping oil field pipe. When I met him, he was rolling in money.

"Hell, I'm the luckiest son of a bitch I know," he told me.

He bought himself an airplane and a new Wagoneer, and he bought electric guitars for his sons in Kansas. When he began spending money on my children, buying them new cowboy boots and saddles, I was transfixed; I'd never seen money flow like . . . well, like water. Born in a drought myself, brought up in the hard-luck tradition of the depression, I could no more have spent money the way Bob did than I could have let water run, wasted, out of a tap. And yet, God, I liked to watch him spend it.

Bob had a jester's license to pull off every audacious stunt I might have longed to try but been afraid to all my life. Under his tutelage I learned to pilot a plane. I let him initiate me into the mile-high club in sweet daylight at ten thousand feet, with the plane on automatic pilot through pillows of cumulus; I flew with him to Calgary, to Houston; and I drank with him in petroleum clubs in the blue haze of the Marlboros he chain-smoked. Through him I met the ragtag and bobtail, newly rich and newly busted exotics of the oil patch, and I listened to their boasting, fatalistic stories of success and disaster. After living twenty years of my life in diligence on college campuses, Bob's exuberance, his grasshopper's delight in the sunlit present, flowed through me like an elixir. I loved his soft Kansas voice, just touched with the flat twang of the Oklahoma border, and I loved his blond hair and diamond-blue eyes and his grin, and I loved his loving me.

After he had spent most of his money, he bought farmland north of Havre and gambled all over again on the weather. I married him in 1978. I wasn't worried; I had a good enough job to pay the bills.

I I I I I I I

The trees that used to arch over the streets in the heart of Great Falls have been cut down. Ancient cottonwoods with their upper branches lopped against the rot still cast shade over the rambling old residences in the central district, but the Great Falls Clinic abuts the pavement and seems to levitate in the sun. In June of 1982 I used to sit in one of its windowless waiting rooms, stabbing away at a piece of needlepoint and listening to the air-conditioning until I could listen no longer and would heave myself out of the chair and limp through the doors and into the scorching heat.

Across from the clinic was a sandwich shop called the Graham Cracker. I would limp across the street and sit at a tiny Formica table where I sipped bitter coffee and listened to the vibrations of another air conditioner and watched the heat shimmer off the cement on the other side of the plate glass until that, too, became intolerable. As I limped back across the street to the clinic my feet felt like hot sponges. I imagined a tiny squirt of fluid out of my sandals with every step I took.

| | | | | | |

A week earlier I had gone to a state humanities committee meeting at Big Sky Resort, south of Bozeman, Montana, and Bob had thrown his golf clubs in the back of my car and gone along. It was a chance for us to have a few days away together, and I looked forward to it. Surely, once he got away from the dust of the highline and his fields of shriveled crops, Bob would be himself again.

But as we turned off the interstate and left the plains, climbing along a highway that follows the Gallatin River where it plunges and dashes from its source, twisting through crags and pines and extravagant outcroppings, Bob grew moody. When we reached the resort and checked into our room, he dropped on the bed and closed his eyes.

"You go ahead," he finally muttered. "I don't want anything to eat."

"Where's Bob?" friends asked when I went down to dinner alone, and I answered, "He isn't feeling well."

I felt more annoyed than alarmed. He had no symptoms that I could see but his inexplicable fatigue. I knew he had fought secret bouts with depression for years, but what was he depressed about?

His crops? But every farmer was a gambler, every farmer faced the perils of drought, blight, rain at the wrong time. When had Bob ever backed away from a gamble?

The baby?

No, I couldn't believe that. But there had always been about Bob a hidden sadness, a deep private well into which the jester sometimes retreated while the face went on smiling.

By lunch the next day he pulled himself together and came downstairs to sit on the terrace under the firs with everyone else, but he had little to say, and when one of my friends made an offhand remark, Bob snarled a retort that briefly stopped all conversation. That evening he would not leave the room at all.

"You need to eat something," I argued. "You missed dinner last night, and again tonight—no wonder you're exhausted."

"I don't want a thing," he said. He lay on the bed with his eyes closed, breathing in short gasps.

"What's wrong?"

"Nothing. I just feel like hell. I'm tired."

"Could you eat if I carried you some soup on a tray?"

"Just let me alone!"

I went downstairs alone. I was angry and frightened. What I had hoped would be a tiny vacation with my husband had turned ugly, and I didn't know why.

The next morning was Saturday. The committee concluded its business and adjourned. Everyone was hurrying back and forth with luggage to check out of the resort by eleven. I went upstairs and let myself into the room with my key. The windows were darkened, and Bob slept, naked, on the bed. His clothing and shaving gear were scattered where he had dropped them.

"Just—lemme rest," he muttered.

I sat down on the bed. "We have to check out."

He opened his eyes, closed them and sighed.

"Do you want me to try to find a doctor?" I asked. We were thirty miles from Bozeman and the nearest medical facilities.

He raised his head off the pillow, let it drop. "Hell no, just—lemme rest a minute."

I sat on the bed a moment longer, trying to decide what to do. I couldn't lift him. He still had, at that time, the frame and weight of the college halfback he once had been, and all 185 pounds of him was inert on the bed. The unreality of it all was defeating me. Call an ambulance? All the way from Bozeman? Surely not. After all, I had seen Bob sink into spells of lassitude before, go into strange fugues of enervation when he seemed incapable of getting out of bed—was this one any different? *Well, yes, it was.* But how?

At last I gathered up the folds of my dress, got up from the bed, and moved slowly around the room, picking up his clothing and packing his shaving kit. Then I made two trips to carry two suitcases down to the lobby, putting my feet carefully down in front of me on stairs I could not see. I brought the car around and parked it in the no-parking zone, as close to the main doors of the resort as I could get it.

"Can you get dressed?" I asked him, back in the darkened room once more.

He roused and nodded. He swung his legs off the bed and then doubled over, his head between his knees.

"Shall I try to find a doctor?" I asked again.

The word *doctor* irritated him into effort. "Don't need a goddamned doctor," he growled, and he sat up and eased his arm into the shirtsleeve I held. Shirt, pants, loafers, and then he stood up, white-faced. Leaning on me, he managed the corridor and the stairs. Once in the lobby, in the sight of other people, he made the effort to straighten and walk by himself out to the car.

I drove down the twisting highway along the Gallatin River while Bob lay back in the passenger seat with his eyes closed. *I'll drive to the emergency room in Bozeman,* I thought. But when I reached the Bozeman exit, I glanced at his face and saw that his color had come back and his breathing was slow and relaxed.

"Hell, keep driving," he said without opening his eyes, and I kept driving.

With the mountains behind us, we drove down through the Gallatin Valley and into the plains. Another thirty miles and we had descended eight thousand feet and come to the little river town of Townsend, halfway between Bozeman and Helena. As I watched the blue outline of the mountains recede in the rearview mirror I thought about Big Sky Resort and the thin cool air at eleven thousand feet above sea level. Bob opened his eyes and sat up in the seat.

"I'm hungry," he said.

I pulled over at a café on Townsend's main street and came around to help him out of the car. His legs were shaky, but he made it into the café and wolfed down a couple of hamburgers.

"Nothing's wrong with me. I just felt like I was worn out," he said.

When we reached Helena, he asked me to pull over and let him drive the rest of the way home.

| | | | | | |

"You've got to see a doctor."

"Hell, nothing's wrong! I been tired."

"You've got to see a doctor!"

"I'll see how I feel after harvest."

"You aren't going to make it through harvest at this rate! Here's the specialist's number. Will you call him, or shall I?"

"Jesus Christ!" he exploded, finally. "If that's what it takes to shut you up—"

| | | | | | |

Our doctor in Havre had sounded shaken. "The X rays show a film over the lungs," he said. "I don't know what it is."

The pulmonary specialist in Great Falls did a series of blood oxygen tests and recommended a lung biopsy.

"Hell no, I ain't letting him go down my throat and snip out a piece of my lungs!"

"But we have to find out what's wrong—"

"Nothing's wrong!"

I raged, begged, pleaded with him until he fled the house for the peace and quiet of the all-night coffee shop. Nothing was the matter with him, just a little fatigue, and he could not understand why I was getting so worked up about nothing. The night I threw myself on the kitchen floor and accused him of deliberately intending to leave me a widow with an unborn child, he was shaken by the state I was in. To quiet me, and not because he believed he was sick, he agreed to the biopsy.

| | | | | | | |

After all those hours of waiting in the Great Falls Clinic came the verdict. Refusing to make eye contact, forcing out his words as though each one came with a price tag, the young specialist explained to us that the film that had shown up on the X rays was pulmonary fibrosis, the incurable, progressive spread of fibrous connective tissues that gradually would choke the capacity of the lungs to take in oxygen and supply it to the body. Bob's blood oxygen level was already about 45 percent, compared with a normal level of 98 percent.

While the growth of the fibroids could not be halted or reversed, the specialist said, it could sometimes be slowed. He recommended a massive therapy of steroids and warned us that mood swings could be among the side effects. Bob should be careful and exact in taking his doses.

"And quit smoking," he told him.

Smoking didn't cause pulmonary fibrosis, although it would exacerbate it. A likely cause was contact with asbestos.

Bob shook his head. Didn't believe he'd ever handled the stuff, he said.

"We may never know where it started," said the specialist, and I wondered why it mattered. He wrote out prescriptions for prednisone and scheduled another appointment in a month's time.

| | | | | | | |

The world must be full of battered souls who stayed on the track because the idea of being run over by a train was more preposterous than the evidence of their own eyes.

For me, the sun rises and another day begins to burn without hope of rain. I pull on a fresh cotton tent dress over my enormous self and cram my feet into sandals and drive to the office for another day of the trivia that pester a college campus in the summer. I cannot believe in September and the end of this pregnancy any more than I can believe in the finality of breath. Bob seems himself these days. More than himself. The steroids have infused him with energy.

"Yeah, I'm runnin' on Prestone," he tells his friends at first.

But he does not like the idea of his body being altered in ways he cannot control by these opaque white pills. When he begins to tinker with his dosage, he drives me nearly crazy with apprehension. Feeling better one day, he takes half his pills. Worse the next, he takes double.

"But the doctor warned us about exact dosages!" I scream.

"Hell, that doc doesn't know a goddamned thing about the way I feel."

"What about the cigarettes?"

"I'll quit after harvest."

In my own way I am as certain as Bob that I can control the invisible menace growing in his lungs. Take the medication, follow the doctor's instructions to the letter, and the menace will be slowed, perhaps for years, and meanwhile we can live as we always have, going our separate ways by day and holding each other by night, delighting in each other's pulse and breath, looking forward to the baby.

Bob's denial, on the other hand, is less complex.

"I don't know why, but the prednisone has stopped working," says the specialist on our next visit to the Great Falls Clinic. "I'm going to start you on interferon. It's a drug used in transplant cases to break down the body's natural immune system, and it must be monitored with extreme care."

I listen, panicky, to his instructions. Was Bob's tinkering with his prednisone dosage the reason for its failure to slow the growth of his fibrosis? What will he do with this potential dynamite? What can I do about it?

On the way home, I find out.

"Hell," he says flatly. "I ain't gonna touch that shit. I'm going to wait until after harvest, and then"—he takes his eyes off the road, looks squarely at me—"then I'm going find out what the hell it is I'm allergic to."

| | | | | | |

Rachel was born at the end of September, and Bob drove us home from the hospital through the last blaze of autumnal color. I carried her into the nursery I had furnished and laid her, sleeping, in her crib. Bob dropped down in a chair beside the crib without taking off his coat or gloves. He watched as she slept: the transparent eyelids of the newborn, the little fists thrown back on either side of her head, the rise and fall of her tiny chest. When I looked in an hour later, neither Rachel nor Bob had moved.

But he had begun to lose weight. Down to 175, then 165 pounds. He bruised easily. Once, while he was holding Rachel, her little fist flailed out and nicked his face with a fingernail, and blood seeped down his cheek for an hour.

He refused to see the specialist again, or any other doctor, but I gleaned information about the progress of his disease where I could find it. "It's the fibrosis that causes the weight loss," explained Rachel's pediatrician when I took her in for her six weeks' checkup. "His body can't maintain itself."

But what caused the mood swings? Was it last summer's dosage of prednisone, still wreaking its roller-coaster damage on his reactions? Was he depressed over an illness he insisted he'd been misdiagnosed with? Or had the dark impulse run within Bob from the beginning, hidden until the combination of drugs and debilitation broke down his defenses? Which was the real Bob?

| | | | | | |

How much financial havoc can a man cause when he sets a farming operation into motion and then watches as through a haze of detachment while fields go uncultivated, obligations unmet, notes unrenewed? How many additional difficulties can he bring down around his shoulders as well as his family's when he fails to file his corporation reports? His FICA and W-4 forms? What if he fails to file his income taxes? Answer: more difficulties than I ever dreamed possible.

I lay awake at two, three, four o'clock in the morning while birch twigs brushed against the bedroom window and cast a maze of shadows as complex and random as the maze my life had become. Hundreds of thousands of dollars whirred through my brain on a squirrel-wheel frequency, organizing themselves into columns and disintegrating to form new totals at rising interest rates. What was I to do? What to do, what to do? Every hope for a way out of the maze was as treacherous as false dawn. The bank would foreclose on the farm in lieu of the $450,000 note? Very well, but the bank would report the transaction to the IRS as a forgiven debt. What, I wondered, did the IRS do with people like me who owed income tax on $450,000? Did they have jails with squirrel wheels in them?

By this time I lay awake alone, usually, in the bed in the shadows of birch twigs. In the mornings I rose and dressed, drove Rachel to her sitter, and hammered away at the solutions that had eluded me in the small hours. By confronting every debt and filing every delinquent report, I could still cling to my illusions. *Face it! Fight it! If we can once deal with the finances, we can still live comfortably on my salary, and surely the disease can be slowed, maybe for years—if you don't believe in the diagnosis, we'll find another specialist. We'll go to Seattle or San Francisco and find another course of treatment, and surely, surely we can buy time, we can have years together. You'll see Rachel grow up—*

But Bob was away from home most of the time now, driven by my frantic tirades and his own denial of the disease that was slowly strangling him. Fired with the idea of getting back into the oil business, of another chance of striking it lucky, he went back to his native Kansas for weeks and then months at a stretch, coming home only to try to raise money for the leases he was buying.

| | | | | | | |

"I found another oil well!"

He looks up from the logbook he has unfolded on the dining room table. Another thirty or forty logbooks are stacked around him or strewn on the floor. Cigarette smoke hangs blue over his head.

"See here? Where the line wavers? I don't see how they could have overlooked it. When they perforated, they missed the zone entirely. I can go in there, unplug it and reperforate, maybe run acid, get the well on stream for fifty, sixty barrels a day, initially—"

Sometimes he finds two or three oil wells in an evening.
"—cost?"

His eyes go opaque for an instant, as though my question
has traveled on some dim transmission from outer space.

"What? The cost to rework one well? Hell, I don't know,
honey, it'd be just one part of my program—twelve wells,
say, at fifteen or twenty thousand— Hell, the cost of one well
don't make no nevermind. I'll be talking to my old buddy
the banker when I go back to Kansas next week. Now, can
you see this? This jiggle on the graph? That's another oil-
producing zone they missed when they finished this well—"

I I I I I I I

"Honey, I realize you don't know a goddamn thing about
the oil business, but I don't understand why you can't *see* it!
Hell, it's right there on the log! And fifty, sixty barrels a day,
even at thirteen dollars a barrel—"

He's down to 150 pounds now. His skin has shrunken over
his cheekbones, and his nails are cyanosed. Still, he's drawing
on some invisible source of energy; his eyes are huge, his
voice urgent as he stabs out one cigarette, lights another, and
uses it to gesture at his logbook. All he needs to get on his
feet again is a few thousand dollars I have in a savings account. Listening to his fevered chatter, I feel drawn into his
dream, his certainty that out there somewhere, in the next
fold of the graph, the next thousand feet of well pipe, is the
ultimate fountainhead of wealth and health. I could drift with
him, believe in him . . . *It was the drought, it was the farm
crisis that bankrupted us, it wasn't his fault—and he knows
the oil business, knows what he's talking about, it's just a
matter of giving him his chance—*

But no.

He flies into a rage at my refusal. "You make me want to
puke! *Puke! Puke! Puke! Puke! Puke!*"

A week of verbal bludgeoning is more than enough. I hand over the money, and he sets off for Kansas, serene in his knowledge that the next throw of the dice is his.

A month later he calls home, jabbering, ecstatic. His old buddy the banker believes in him.

"It's growing on trees down here! The money's growing on trees!"

| | | | | | |

We don't hear from him after that. Another spring deepens into another hot summer, and the lawns and evergreens in Havre suffer the stress from curtailed watering. After work I pick Rachel up from her sitter's and play with her in the swing I have hung in the backyard willow. Rachel has seen so little rain in her life that when a brief deceptive shower fits its way overhead and a few raindrops lash the willow leaves, she asks, "What's that, Mom?"

Swing, swing, every day a bead on a string. Take Rachel to the sitter's and go to work in the mornings, pick her up and come home at night, swing her in the swing and bathe her and feed her and put her to bed. A whiskey and a book and Emmylou Harris for me. Swing, swing, the phone doesn't ring.

"Why don't you divorce him?" one of the attorneys had asked last summer.

This summer I file for divorce.

| | | | | | |

"Honey, *why?*"

In the hum of the long-distance line between Montana and Kansas, I try to think why.

"I'm coming home," he says after the silence. "I don't really have the time, I got a well just coming into production, but I can see you ain't left me no other choice."

Rachel and I drive to Great Falls to meet him at the airport. I recognize the man who appears on the ramp by his fair hair. He walks a step or two, gasps for breath. A ghost's eyes glow at us.

"Sure missed my two honeys," says the ghost. "Sure hated being away."

One of the disembarking flight attendants touches my arm. "Something's really wrong with this man," she says. "He's having terrible trouble breathing."

I nod.

She hesitates, glancing over our small sick circle. "Well— just so somebody knows," she says finally, and hurries off with her flight bag rolling behind her on its little wheels.

Rachel cuddles up to him. "My honey," he says, teary-eyed.

When we reach the car, he gets in the driver's seat and lights a cigarette. "We'll get rid of this pig," he says, "and buy you a new Lincoln as soon as the well comes on stream. They got new dealers' models in Kansas for under twenty thou. Helluva deal. There's a house down there I want you to see. It's an estate, actually."

"Let me drive."

"Hell, I feel fine! Long as I stay on my medication, I'm fine."

"Medication?"

"My Primatene Mist."

| | | | | | |

"The banker here in Havre don't want to make me a loan. He says he heard you've filed for divorce. But I told him you're dropping the action. You are dropping the action, aren't you?"

Hell, we got no problems, honey!

If only I could suspend my disbelief, accept the invitation

to waltz with this rattling skeleton. But I hear him shouting into the phone at someone in Kansas: *It's still pumping water? Guess we'll have to go down further and shoot the second zone! What? Hell, I don't know! I'm planning to come back down to Kansas by the end of the week! At least by Monday! Hell yes, you'll get paid!*

"I'm having to sue my old buddy the banker for that sixty thousand he still owes me," he explains. "Sonovabitch got cold feet. Hell, can't blame him, in a sense. He don't know a goddamn thing about the oil patch."

No, I won't descend any further with him into his shadow world. I'll murder him instead with disbelief. From the light's edge I will watch as he walks under dead trees where dreams hang like leaves, as he fades into transparency and gibbers at me from the dim reaches: *It sure makes me feel good to know how much confidence my wife's got in me, Mary!*

| | | | | | |

"You've got to get him out of the house," says the attorney.

You try to divorce me, and you'll never see that little girl again, Mary! Hell no, I'm not talking about custody! I'm just telling you, Mary! You'll never see her again!

"But how can I take him seriously?" I plead.

"We have to take his threats seriously," says the attorney.

The second or third time the police have to come and drag him out of the house, the attorney applies to the judge for a restraining order. So he hides behind a hedge in a borrowed car until a new neighbor comes running across the street: "Quick! A man's trying to coax your little girl into his car with him!"

"We can't put him in jail," says the police lieutenant. "My God, the man's on oxygen."

I don't know why you can't see it, Mary! Hell, that lawyer's just running up his fees. I know I can't tell you a goddamn thing. You think you know it all. But eventually you're going to find out—

I have my phone number changed, and changed again, and still there comes at midnight or one A.M. the single ring. I pick it up to dial tone or to the hesitant whisper: *Honey? Hell, I'll forgive you. I just don't understand how you could throw me out.*

He has hired himself an attorney by now, and the paperwork blizzards back and forth. He demands a division of property, a maintenance allowance, and custody of Rachel. But when it comes to settlement, he backs off; when a hearing date is set, he calls the judge and gets an extension. What he really wants is not to be divorced.

"We could leave it like this," says the attorney finally, wearily. "You have a restraining order and temporary child custody, pending settlement. And you're leaving Montana in a month or two."

So it will never end.

"You don't think he'd try to follow you?" the attorney asks.

"I think he's too sick to follow far."

| | | | | | |

He lives in a room in the Havre Hotel. Bed, dresser, air-conditioning unit in the window. He can sit in the lobby downstairs and watch TV or watch the traffic on First Street. He can walk around the corner to PJ's Lounge and play a little poker, but he has to carry his portable oxygen supply everywhere he goes. He's a walking skeleton. He has nothing to do, nothing to look forward to—How could she have done it to him?

| | | | | | |

No, it will never end. Not with the ringing of a telephone, three Octobers later in the golden Palouse. Not when I agree with his sister that yes, we should lay him beside his parents; yes, I will want to bring Rachel. And it will not end with the late-night flight into Wichita, and not with the familiar faces of my kind brother-in-law and his wife waiting to drive us through the murky country roads to the small-town parlor where he waits. Rachel goes wild in the car, kicking, struggling; but when we get to Little River, she calms down and walks up the porch steps and through the door with its oval of Victorian glass.

"Why are his eyes shut?"

It is the first time I have seen him in the flesh since that day three years ago, just before I left Montana for good, when he cornered me in public and ranted, raged, finally slapped my face with all the feeble fury he could muster at my refusal to his waltz. For a moment I fight off the irrational feeling that, sensing my presence, he will sit up in his coffin, chattering, his ghost's eyes glowing: *Why, Mary? Why?*

"How old are you?" the Methodist minister asks Rachel.

"Seven," she whispers.

The Little River cemetery holds the only high ground for miles, and the grass is as stiff and sere as it would be in Montana in October. The wind snarls at the grass and roars in the canopy they have pitched over the open grave, and I remember another cemetery ridge a long time ago, and another dry-eyed woman named Mary.

At the end they fold the flag and hand it to me, the technical widow; and I turn as prearranged and hand it to one of his sons. No, it never ends. Perhaps my grandmother could have told me that. Her shade follows, as does his, through the windswept grass as Rachel and I walk hand in hand down the gravel track from the knoll.

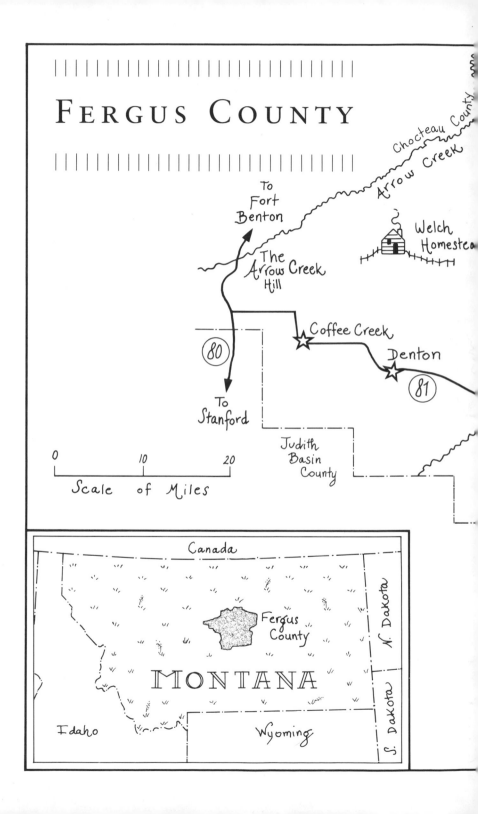